DOUBLEDAY
POCKET
BIBLE
GUIDE

Linda L. Grenz

DOUBLEDAY

NEW YORK   LONDON   TORONTO
SYDNEY   AUCKLAND

PUBLISHED BY DOUBLEDAY, a division of Bantam Doubleday Dell
Publishing Group, Inc.
1540 Broadway, New York, New York 10036

DOUBLEDAY and the portrayal of an anchor with a dolphin are
trademarks of Doubleday, a division of Bantam Doubleday Dell
Publishing Group, Inc.

Scripture quotations are from the *New Revised Standard Version*
copyright © 1989, by The Division of Christian Education of the
National Council of the Churches of Christ in the U.S.A.
Finding Help in the Bible (page 177) is adapted from the "Special
Reader's Helps" in the *New American Standard Bible,* copyright ©
1991, by the American Bible Society, and used with permission.
Revised Common Lectionary, copyright © 1992 by the Consultation
on Common Texts (CCT). Used with permission.

Book Design by Stanley S. Drate/Folio Graphics Co., Inc.

Library of Congress Cataloging-in-Publication Data

Grenz, Linda L., 1950–
    Doubleday pocket Bible guide / Linda L. Grenz. —
1st ed.
      p. cm.
    Includes bibliographical references.
    1. Bible—Introductions.   I. Title.
    BS475.2.G68   1997
    220.6'1—dc21   96-39381
                                         CIP

ISBN 0-385-48568-9
Copyright © 1997 by Linda L. Grenz
All Rights Reserved
Printed in the United States of America
First Edition

10 9 8 7 6 5 4 3 2 1

ACKNOWLEDGMENTS

This book would not have been written without the vision and dedication of Chuck Stetson, director and publisher of the Center for Christian Formation, and the unfaltering cheers of Nina Frost, marketing director. The Center for Christian Formation sponsored this project as part of their efforts to develop basic resources on Christianity for seekers and learners. Information about the center's materials and on-line courses is available at http://www.ccfonline.com.

Thomas May, director of the National Bible Association, also provided valuable encouragement and support during the writing process. Bruce Campbell and Joseph Russell provided editorial assistance in the development of the original draft. Thanks to my editor, Mark Fretz, for shaping this project into a useful book, for creating the Time Line (pp. 291–97), and for editing the maps (pp. 299–309).

AN
INVITATION

What is my purpose in life? How do I make sense of what takes place in the world around me? What does God have in store for me? Why do terrible things sometimes happen to good people?

These ago-old questions haunt and intrigue us. They lead us to seek answers in ancient words and sacred truths, just as millions of people have been doing for centuries. Such questions lead many of us to the Bible, a sacred book that we trust will speak powerfully to our deepest needs.

Many of us own a Bible, but not many of us read it. Most of us know, somewhere deep within, that the words of God have the power to make a vital, lasting difference in our lives. But finding the Word of God in the Bible's many words may seem daunting, even overwhelming.

The *Doubleday Pocket Bible Guide* will help you find what you need in the Bible. Whether you choose to read the Bible alone or with a family member, whether you study it with a colleague from work or with a fellow member of your church or synagogue, the *Doubleday Pocket Bible Guide* can give your exploration new depth and clarity. It will open up a host of ways you can use to learn from the Bible. May using this book help you along in the adventure of reading the Bible!

CONTENTS

SECTION I
GETTING STARTED

SECTION II
EXPLORING THE BIBLE

SECTION III

FURTHERING YOUR UNDERSTANDING

SECTION IV

AIDS TO STUDY

SECTION

I

GETTING
STARTED

THE BOOK OF YOUR LIFE

Countless people have found that the Bible has a unique and compelling power to describe and renew their lives. It helps them understand themselves or make important decisions. It offers hope, encouragement, and a sense of peace. It tells them that no matter who they are or what they have done, God reaches out in love.

Even some of the "boring" parts of the Bible give people clues to what life is about. The Bible tells a story that is familiar and yet new to each person who reads it. It tells the story of your life and mine. It tells the story of people who have followed and been met by God. And it tells God's story. You don't have to know anything about the Bible—you don't even have to be especially "religious"—to discover that you and God are closer to each other than you ever imagined.

The common image of life as a journey suggests movement, development, and a willingness to go forward. Our spiritual life is a journey on which we search for someone or something to hold life together and make sense of what we experience. In the Bible, Jews see that "someone or something" as Yahweh; Christians find it in God as revealed in Jesus Christ.

The Bible tells us how God's people have experienced and understood God throughout the centuries and how that experience and understanding changed them. So studying God's Word is a spiritual journey we take with the hosts of people who have gone before us—and millions who travel it each day. We can travel that journey for the rest of our lives and never run out of things to see and learn and explore. Each time we open the Bible, we can discover something new. It is a living book. And one that can continue to speak to us and help us along. In fact, reading the Bible is not as complicated as many think. Understanding God may be more within your reach than you realize. "Ask," said Jesus, "and it will be given you; search, and you will find; knock, and the door will be opened for you" (Matthew 7:7).

I invite you to join me on this journey to discover who God is and who God calls you to be, to find your life story in the Bible's stories and to experience for yourself the power and presence of God's Word in your life. I am a Christian, so my understanding of the Bible and my witness to its power in my life grows out of that perspective. People of other faiths will find much of the Bible's story is their story as well. Christians, Jews, and Muslims, in particular, share a common biblical heritage that can be explored together. Those who are not members of any particular faith but are drawn to the power of sacred scriptures will also find the Bible to be a place where they can meet the Holy One.

What's In It?

The Bible is the story of God's action in the world, and it tells God's Word for all people. Not just one book, it is rather a rich and fascinating library of books. This library contains stories about the high and low moments of life, about heroes and villains, battles and travels, prophets and rulers. It compiles songs and poems, and long lists of genealogies and regulations. It chronicles stories of the life of Jesus and his earliest followers, along with letters written to friends or groups of Christians that met in homes. And it is replete with more general guidelines for living.

> *For whatever was written in former days was written for our instruction, so that by steadfastness and by the encouragement of the scriptures we might have hope.*
>
> —Romans 15:4

Like the volumes in any library, the Bible's books were written by different people at different times and places. Some books were written by several people. Sometimes more than one person wrote about the same story in different books. These stories were not written down as they happened; they were told over and over, often for generations, before someone finally put pen to paper (or papyrus!). As best as scholars can tell, the various books of the Bible were penned during a thousand-year period that began as far back as three thousand years ago. So the Bible comes to us through many people whose lives spanned many years.

The Bible has been many things to different readers since it was written. So too, each of us reads and experiences the Bible differently depending on who we are and what is happening in our lives.

For many people the Bible has been:

- A source of comfort in difficult times. War veterans, prisoners, hostages, and those who are ill, in great pain, or facing death often tell of turning to the Bible to understand their suffering and to find strength to face what is ahead of them. (See "Finding Help in the Bible," p. 177, for helpful passages.)
- A treasury of familiar stories for children and adults: Joseph and his coat of many colors; Noah and the ark; Moses leading the Hebrew people from slavery in Egypt to the Promised Land; King David's adultery with Bathsheba; Queen Esther's bravery; Ruth's loyalty; the birth, life, death, and resurrection of Jesus; and the stories

about Paul and the early church. These stories are so popular because in them we see the goodness and the failures of both average people and royalty. And in them we can see ourselves.

- A guide for living well and wisely. The "rules of life" that emerge from the stories, the Ten Commandments and the Torah, Christ's Great Commandment, the words of wisdom told by leaders of old, the passage on love in 1 Corinthians 13, all have helped people understand how to live holier lives.

- A collection of profound insights about our identity. The Bible tells us who we are as people of God. To find ourselves, we do more than look inward, we also turn to the wisdom of the biblical ancients.

Take It Personally

To fully understand the Bible, what we read there must be personal and relevant to our lives. What we find there must tell us about God and what it means to be a person of God. And we study the Bible with others so we can tell stories from our own spiritual journeys, hear the stories of others, and find those stories echoed in the lives of people ancient and contemporary. In this way we hear God's Word and together learn to live as God's holy people in today's world.

For both Christians and Jews, the Bible is the story of God's faithful relationship with people over centuries.

For Jews, the Bible relates how they became God's chosen people, were brought to the Promised Land, and led into a covenant relationship with God. Jews study the Bible to learn and heed "the Law" (Torah, instruction). This spells out the terms of the covenant relationship between God and the Israelites and continues to guide them on how they are called to live as the people of God.

For Christians, the Bible also contains the story of God's ultimate act of bringing people into full relationship with God through the life, death, and resurrection of Jesus Christ.

> *For God so loved the world that he gave his only Son, so that everyone who believes in him may not perish but may have eternal life.*
>
> —John 3:16

Christians study the story of God's action through Christ so that we can become part of that story—entering into full relationship with God through Christ. We understand that our relationship with God is not ours alone; it is in and through Christ and other Christians.

You may be a Christian, a Jew, a member of another faith group, or you may not belong to any organized religion. You can find help and meaning in the Bible in your own way and in your own faith group. Just open the book and read. And look around you; you will find a fellow traveler who will go on the journey with you.

USING THIS BOOK

This pocket guide gives you several simple ways to read and study the Bible. It is divided into sections:

- "Books of the Bible" gives a summary of the contents and an outline of every book in the Bible to help you select what you want to study. It also lists famous passages in each book. This section is divided into three parts:
  - ▶ Old Testament (also referred to as the Hebrew Scriptures, Jewish Bible, or Tanakh)
  - ▶ Apocrypha (also known as the Deuterocanonical Scriptures)
  - ▶ New Testament (also called the Christian Testament)

- "Approaches to Scripture" provide a wide variety of step-by-step plans to help you lead a group in reading the Scriptures or to do your own reading, reflection, and study. These include:
  - ▶ "Finding Your Way," which lays out what you will see when you open the book
  - ▶ "Individual Approaches to Scripture"
  - ▶ "Family Approaches to Scripture"
  - ▶ "Group Approaches to Scripture"
  - ▶ "Finding Help in the Bible," which leads you to verses on various topics, emotions, or situations

- ▸ "The Complete Revised Common Lectionary," which gives you a course of readings you can use as the basis of a weekly reading or study session

- "People in the Bible" and "Places in the Bible" tell you about the most common people and places in the Bible
- "Glossary of Terms" defines key words and concepts you will find in the Bible that may be unfamiliar
- The Time Line and maps give a chronology of the key events in the books of the Bible along with maps of biblical lands at various points in history
- "Tools for Further Study" lists some basic references to keep your exploration going.

So pick a passage and/or an approach that best suits you. (See "Your Personality and Scripture" on p. 173 for descriptions of personality types and their relationship to the various methods of approaching the Bible.) Use the descriptions in "Books of the Bible," "The Complete Revised Common Lectionary," or the topics list, "Finding Help in the Bible," to select a place to begin. But the best way to start is to do just that: begin!

BOOKS OF THE BIBLE

The Bible is composed of two major sections: the Old Testament and the New Testament. Some versions of the Bible also include the Apocrypha as a separate section.

Many people today call the Old Testament Hebrew Scriptures or the Jewish Bible in recognition that these books of the Bible, written before the time of Jesus, were and are the Scriptures of the Hebrew or Jewish people. Likewise, the New Testament is often referred to as the Christian Testament in recognition that it bears witness to the Christian story. The Apocrypha (which means "hidden things") is a collection of books that some accept as part of the Bible while others do not. Some versions of the Bible call them the apocryphal/deuterocanonical books.[1]

Because the Bible assembles into one volume many books that have been written over centuries and in many different places, there is no single way to arrange those books "on the shelf." The arrangement of books we have used is found in most versions of the Christian Bible. However, the Jewish Bible and some versions of the Christian Bible follow a different arrangement. This is because the Jewish and Christian communities spent many years deciding which books to include in the canon (official list) and various groups came to different conclusions.

[1]The word *deuterocanonical* means "second canon."

While these groups hold a significant amount of Scripture in common, there are these differences:

- Hebrew-speaking Jews accepted the list of twenty-four books now identified as the Hebrew Scriptures perhaps as early as the second century BCE.[2] After the destruction of the temple in 70 CE rabbis engaged in debates that settled any lingering questions by the end of the first century CE.

- Greek-speaking Jews translated the Greek Bible (known as the Septuagint), which contained a longer list that included many of the books now in the Apocrypha. The Greek Bible and its list of books was later abandoned in Judaism, while it was adopted by Christians.

- The Roman Catholic Church adopted this longer list as their canon for the Old Testament at the Council of Trent in 1546; it is also the list used by the Eastern Orthodox churches.

- The Protestant and Anglican (Episcopal) churches generally accepted the shorter list (i.e., the Hebrew Scriptures) as a source of doctrine. Martin Luther included the Apocrypha as an appendix to his 1534 German translation, setting the pattern for most Protestant editions of the Bible.[3]

- Meanwhile, the canon of the New Testament was generally agreed upon by all Christians by the end of the fourth century (although the Eastern Orthodox churches continue some debate on some portions to this day).

Today most Protestant Bibles have thirty-nine books in the Old Testament, while most Roman Catholic Bibles list forty-six books (adding many, but not all, of the books of the Apocrypha). Both have twenty-seven books in the New Testament. Some versions of the Bible include the

---

[2]*The New Interpreter's Bible*, Volume I, p. 9; BCE is an abbreviation for "Before the Common Era"; CE for "Common Era," referring to the time held in common by Christians, Jews, and Muslims. BCE refers to the time before the birth of Christ.

[3]*The New Interpreter's Bible*, Volume I, p. 12.

fifteen books in the Apocrypha as a separate section between the Old and New Testaments or at the end of the New Testament; others omit it entirely. The Hebrew Bible used by the Jews (called the Old Testament in the Christian Bible) has twenty-four books (or twenty-two if you count some of the combination books as one).[4]

Divisions of the Hebrew Scriptures (Old Testament)

The simplest way to grasp the order of the books of the Bible is to look at the Bible's table of contents. However, Jewish and Christian Bibles arrange the books of the Hebrew Bible (Old Testament) in a different order. The Jewish Bible is divided into three major sections:

1

THE LAW

(Torah, sometimes translated as "teaching" or "instruction")

- Genesis ("In the beginning")[5]
- Exodus ("Names")
- Leviticus ("And he called")
- Numbers ("In the wilderness")
- Deuteronomy ("Words")

---

[4]The number of books in the Bible is confusing because some versions of the Bible count books with two parts (e.g. 1 and 2 Kings) as two books while others count them as one book. And some compilers believe Ezra and Nehemiah should be two separate books, while others see them as two parts of a single book.

[5]In the Hebrew Bible the books are often named using the opening words or the key words in the book. The English titles are generally based on titles in the Septuagint, the ancient Greek translation of the Hebrew Scriptures.

2
THE PROPHETS

THE EARLY PROPHETS

- Joshua
- Judges
- 1 and 2 Samuel
- 1 and 2 Kings

THE LATER PROPHETS

- Isaiah
- Jeremiah
- Ezekiel
- Hosea
- Joel
- Amos
- Obadiah
- Jonah
- Micah
- Nahum
- Habakkuk
- Zephaniah
- Haggai
- Zechariah
- Malachi

3
THE WRITINGS

- Psalms ("Praises")
- Proverbs
- Job
- The Song of Solomon (Also called The Song of Songs)
- Ruth
- Lamentations ("How")
- Ecclesiastes ("Preacher")

- Esther
- Daniel
- Ezra–Nehemiah
- 1 and 2 Chronicles

Divisions of the Christian Bible

The Greek-speaking Jews, especially those living in Alexandria, Egypt, translated the Hebrew Scriptures into Greek and rearranged the books after the Pentateuch (which means "five scrolls") according to literary types. This is the order used by Christian Bibles (books in the Apocrypha, which are italicized below, are often found in a separate section).[6]

1

PENTATEUCH

- Genesis
- Exodus
- Leviticus
- Numbers
- Deuteronomy

2

NARRATIVE/HISTORY

- Joshua
- Judges

[6]These books are included in the Roman Catholic and Orthodox Bibles but not in Protestant Bibles, which may include them in a noncanonical section (the Apocrypha). The apocryphal books are not considered part of the canon of the Jewish Bible. The books of Esther and Daniel are longer in the Roman Catholic versions than in Protestant or Jewish Bibles (extra sections are found in the Apocrypha). And the Prayer of Manasseh, not part of the Roman Catholic Bible, is included in some versions of the Apocrypha.

- Ruth
- 1 and 2 Samuel
- 1 and 2 Kings
- 1 and 2 Chronicles
- *1 Esdras* (Greek for Ezra)
- *2 Esdras*

3

POETIC AND DIDACTIC BOOKS

- Psalms
- Proverbs
- Ecclesiastes
- The Song of Solomon
- Job
- *The Wisdom of Solomon*
- *Ecclesiasticus*

4

STORIES

- Esther (with *Additions*)
- *Judith*
- *Tobit*

5

PROPHETS

- Isaiah
- Jeremiah
- *Baruch*
- Lamentations
- *Epistle of Jeremiah*
- Ezekiel
- Daniel (with *Additions*)

THE TWELVE
- Hosea
- Joel
- Amos
- Obadiah
- Jonah
- Micah
- Nahum
- Habakkuk
- Zephaniah
- Haggai
- Zechariah
- Malachi

6

INTERTESTAMENTAL HISTORY

- *1 and 2 Maccabees*

THE BIBLE IS A STORYBOOK

When reading the Bible, it is important to remember that it is a written version of oral stories. Some of these storytelling devices are familiar. Others feel unfamiliar to modern readers. Repetition, exaggeration for effect, dramatic dialogue, imagery, and symbols were all accepted tools for "telling the story." For example, "forty days" was a common expression that meant "a long time" rather than a literal forty days. Sometimes you may need to do a bit of sleuthing to find out what a word or phrase meant to the original writers. After all, we often use language differently today than the ancients did.

Remember also that the "authors" of these books were not professional writers or scholars. They were often anonymous people whose writings were later given the name of some famous and respected person. In some cases there were multiple writers, a sort of committee with a scribe. In most cases the materials were compiled, edited, and even translated several times by a number of people over many years. All of this created opportunities for translation errors, divergent interpretations, and the like. But what is amazing is not that we can find variations in the texts, but rather how accurately the written record has come down through the centuries.[7]

[7]In 1947 jars containing ancient manuscripts of the Bible were dis-

This raises the question of "divine inspiration." How people understand God's role in inspiring the Holy Scriptures varies greatly, but most people of faith fall into three broad groups:

- Those who believe that God oversaw the writing of the texts to such an extent that every word and fact is correct and true (terms like *inerrant* or *infallible* are often used for the Bible)
- Those who believe God inspired or guided the Scriptures but that human persons wrote and translated them and thereby introduced human perspectives and even errors. People in this group tend to see such mistakes as minor and not impinging on significant truths.
- Those who believe that we find in the Bible God's enduring truths but that these need to be read through a modern lens. People in this group argue that statements of the Bible need to be restated in ways more comprehensible to modern people.

Many believe, as do I, that while God inspired the Bible's writing, that inspiration has not kept the people involved from occasional mistakes. Why else would a God who knows all things "write" several versions of the same story with points in one that conflict with the other? That in no way precludes, however, God's inspiring of those who wrote down and even translated those words.

Members of each faith group or community have to decide how they view God's role in the writing of Scripture. And ultimately each individual also has to decide. You may choose to follow the direction of your faith group or community, seek the advice of a respected teacher, or you may use your own research and wisdom to decide.

covered. Known as the Dead Sea Scrolls, they are now being translated and reveal a remarkable similarity to the texts as we have them today.

FINDING YOUR WAY

When you open the Bible you will immediately see that it does not look like any other book you've read. So before you launch into it, consider this brief guided tour:

Chapter and Verse

First, the books of the Bible have been somewhat arbitrarily divided into chapters and verses. These divisions were not original; they were added to help people find a specific sentence in the Bible quickly and easily.

Each sentence, or part of a sentence, has a number; this is the verse number. The chapters are numbered too. When you see a reference like John 3:16 (or 3.16), John refers to the name of the book, three refers to the chapter, and sixteen refers to the verse. If you see the reference 3:16–18, it refers to verse sixteen through verse eighteen. Sometimes you will see it as 3:16a, which refers to just the first half of verse sixteen.

People refer to a verse or group of verses as "a Scripture passage" or just "a passage." It's not clear why that term came to be applied to a selection from a book, but it works. You may also hear people refer to a verse or group of verses as "a text" from the Scriptures.

This system of numbered chapters and verses helps you to find a specific sentence quickly and easily. This is especially important since every version of the Bible has different page numbers, making it extremely difficult to find a particular sentence otherwise.

Some versions of the Bible give a chapter title, or they may have subtitles that give the topic for a section. These will be different in every Bible because they are added to the text either by the translators or publishers of that edition. In some cases these numbers and titles may be more confusing or bothersome than helpful, so feel free to skip over them.

Titles and Table of Contents

The title of each book is not what we usually expect in a book title. Usually the title is one word (Mark) that refers to the primary readers (Corinthians), the writer (Luke), the name of the key person (Ruth), event (Exodus), or class of people (Kings). Those titles were given to different books over time, not by the first writers. So they don't convey the kind of information we expect in a title. Some books have longer versions of their titles printed in the book, but most people refer to the book by the one-word title. Exceptions are books that have 1 or 2 (sometimes I or II) before their titles, which are identified as First and Second Kings, and so on.

Most Bibles feature a list of the books and their starting page numbers in the front. But there is no standard table of contents you can skim to see what is in a book. That's one of the reasons this guide gives you an outline and a few verses to help you get an overview of each book.

SECTION

II

EXPLORING
THE BIBLE

THE HEBREW SCRIPTURES

(commonly known as the Old Testament)

The Old Testament is a collection of books written between the twelfth and second century BCE primarily in Hebrew. These diverse books comprise the Jewish Bible (Tanakh) for Jews and the Old Testament or Hebrew Scriptures for Christians. Tradition divides the *Tanakh* into Law (or Hebrew *tôrâ*—T), Prophets (or Hebrew *nebi'im*—N), and Writings (or Hebrew *Khethubim*—Kh).

The Law: The Core Narrative of the Hebrew Scriptures

The first five books of the Bible are known as the Pentateuch (literally, "five scrolls") or the Torah. They tell the oldest stories of the Hebrew people. The Torah forms the core of Hebrew scriptures—everything else is built on its central themes and structure.

Like the Christian Scriptures, the Pentateuch tells a sacred history. Its reverent themes have been recited again and again. Then they were reinterpreted, expanded, and passed along to the next generation. The promises to Israel's patriarchs, God's deliverance of the Hebrews from slavery in Egypt, the giving of the Law at Mount Sinai, God's guidance and faithful provision during Israel's wilderness wanderings, and their inheritance of the Promised Land all crowd the pages of the Bible's first five books.

Crucial to understanding these key events are covenants, agreements that carried immense freight in biblical times. They signified formal promises through a verbal oath or a symbolic action (sign). Some were conditional, others unconditional. Especially important to the Bible were covenants between God and a person or the people. The Torah portrays God as a covenant-making God, as one willing to bind himself to his people. It describes three primary covenants between God and God's people:

- God's unconditional covenant with Noah that "never again shall there be a flood to destroy the earth" (Genesis 9). The rainbow was to be a sign of this covenant, which was "for all future generations."
- God's unconditional promise to give Abraham and his descendants the Promised Land (Genesis 15 and 17). The practice of male circumcision formed the primary and most lasting sign of this covenant.
- The conditional covenant between God and the people of Israel at Mount Sinai when God gave Moses the Ten Commandments (Exodus 19–20) with the expectation that the people would "keep God's laws" in exchange for which God promises to be their God.

"Remember" is an often repeated word in the Pentateuch. The covenants and great events of Israel's story were not to be forgotten. This is how the stories of families and nations are developed; it was also how the stories of the Hebrew Bible came to be our sacred stories. Only after that process is complete or nearly complete did someone finally write it all down.

Since the Hebrew Scriptures repeat the same stories several times from different perspectives, consider how a story is formed and becomes part of our history and understanding of reality:

1. something happens;
2. a people reflects on the event and draws significance from it;

3. people repeat and repeat again the story in a way that reflects the significance of the event for them;

4. the story finds expression in liturgy, ballad, poetry, drama, music;

5. the story becomes central to creed, worldview, and formalized beliefs.[1]

Not surprisingly, not all the Pentateuch's storytellers shared the same perspective. While all agreed that God was acting on behalf of the people, certain individuals and groups wanted to highlight events in slightly different ways. And because the stories and precepts were told orally for many centuries before being written, we can detect different strands of influence in the stories we now have. Scholars identify four perspectives or groups of storytellers within the Pentateuch:

1. The J source reflects its Judean (southern Israelite) roots in the time of the early Hebrew monarchy (c. 950 BCE). This writer or writers called God *Yahweh* or *Jahweh*[2] (thus the J designation) and was especially interested in Abraham and David. J material tells the story of the Hebrew people by presenting the kings as descendants of Abraham and as administrators of the covenant with Moses (known as the Mosaic covenant).

2. The E source reflects northern Israelite roots (c. 850 BCE) and calls God Elohim. It covers the same story as the J source but because of its roots in the northern kingdom it has more interest in prophecy and Moses

[1]The author is indebted to Joseph Russell for this and the following outline of the story.

[2]God's sacred name appeared as a four-letter word, YHWH, and at various points in history was never pronounced because a person or god's name was considered to contain the person's essence or being. In most cases secondary words such as *Lord* were used to refer to God. Much later in history, vowels were added to the sacred name and it was pronounced Jahweh, Yahweh, or Jehovah. There are various theories about the meaning of the name—the most common is that it means *I am who [or what] I am* (Exodus 3:14). Another verb form of the same word would translate as: *I cause to be what comes into existence.* (*The Interpreter's Dictionary of the Bible,* Volume 2, pages 407–417).

and less interest in Jerusalem, King David, and his descendants.

3. The D (Deuteronomic) source reflects the time of King Josiah's reform of the people amid their waning commitment to keeping God's laws (621 BCE). It is best seen in the book of Deuteronomy and probably was written after 650 BCE.

4. The P (Priestly) source focuses on how to worship and tells the story from the perspective of those affiliated with the liturgy.[3] It comes from the time after the people were exiled to Babylonia (after 550 BCE).

These different strands of tradition were woven together in various stages until the first five books were established and accepted as Holy Scripture in about 400 BCE.

Types of Books in the Hebrew Scriptures

If events are central to the Pentateuch as a whole, they are also pivotal to particular books in the whole of the Hebrew Scriptures. Here are the "headline" events of Israelite narrative along with the books in which they are chronicled:

1. God orchestrates the Exodus—perhaps the most pivotal event of Hebrew history (Exodus);

2. God institutes the Sinai covenant, which established the identity-forming worldview of the Jews (Exodus, Leviticus, Numbers, Deuteronomy);

3. the Hebrew people settle in Canaan (Joshua and Judges);

4. they are ruled by judges (Judges), then

5. three great kings—Saul, David, and Solomon (1 and 2 Samuel–1 Kings 11)

6. the nation is divided into two parts and prophets reflect on the implications (1 Kings 12 through 2 Kings 17, Amos, and Jeremiah);

[3]For more information see *The Oxford Study Bible,* pages 7–9 and *The Interpreter's Dictionary of the Bible,* Supplementary Volume, pages 130ff.

7. stories of beginnings and the concept of "a chosen people" in relationship with God are established (Genesis);
8. Jerusalem falls (for the first time) and the people are exiled;
9. they return from exile to partial restoration (Ezra and Nehemiah);
10. they hope for a political messiah (Daniel) and full restoration in the future.

There are several different types of books and literature in the Hebrew Scriptures.

- Narrative material is more like a diary or a record of family stories than a history book. The biblical writers approached their material differently than would a modern historian seeking to chronicle events accurately and "objectively." Narratives record traditional stories and legends, tell events in ways suitable for reciting in public worship, or give accounts in a way that makes a specific point.
- Prophetic literature was written by people understood to be messengers for God. They announced God's assessment of the nation and its leaders and God's action in the immediate future. Their followers or scribes often recorded these announcements.
- Apocalyptic books report a revelation that an angel or otherworldly being has given. Apocalyptic literature is usually about the "end times" (end of the world), although it may also give predictions about what is to happen in the near future.
- Wisdom literature (such as Proverbs) sometimes consists of compilations of wise sayings. It may also take on other, more poetic forms that talk about Divine Wisdom personified in female imagery or presented as the "spirit of God."
- Prayers, hymns, songs, and rituals are liturgical (worship) works, or "prayer books" of the temple and synagogue. They were and still are used during worship services or for private times of prayer and worship.

- Law codes are a form of writing found within several books. They describe the rules of the religion, commandments established by God, or laws decreed by rulers.

Descriptions, Outlines, and Famous Passages

The following descriptions of the books of the Bible are based on information drawn from various sources listed in "Tools for Further Study" (pp. 282–290), including Bibles such as *The Oxford Study Bible*.[4] Each book has a personal "rating system" which will give you an indication of where to start if you are new to the Bible. Read those with one or two dots first and leave those with four or five dots for later or turn to them when searching for a specific story or passage. The rating does not signify the books' importance as much as which are easiest to read, especially for those unfamiliar with the Bible.

Symbols indicate level of difficulty: from ❊ (relatively easy reading) to ❊❊❊❊❊ (difficult reading, for experienced readers).

[4]New York: Oxford University Press, 1992.

THE LAW

GENESIS

NARRATIVE

Genesis tells the story of God's creation of the universe and God's early relationship with humankind. It begins with two complementary stories of creation and establishes how the ideal, Edenic relationship humans had with God was broken. After flooding the earth, God made a covenant with Noah and promised not to flood the earth again.

The second covenant concerns Abram (later renamed Abraham); it promises that he and Sarah would be blessed and have many descendants who would inhabit a land promised by God.[5] Male circumcision was to be the visible sign of this covenant and Isaac was the son born to fulfill the promise. Jews view Abraham as their primary forebear; Christians see him as a key figure in "salvation history," and Muslims look to him as an early prophet. Jews

---

[5]This land became known as the Promised Land and is called Canaan after the Canaanites, who lived there. Today we call it Palestine or Israel.

Before 14,000 BCE	4,200 to 3,300 BCE	2,000 to 1,500 BCE	1,500 to 1,200 BCE	1,200 to 1,150 BCE
Creation Accounts	Noah and the Ark	Patriarchal Age	Hebrews in Egypt	Wilderness Wanderings

and Muslims continue circumcision as a practice having religious significance.

Abraham's faith was tested when God commanded him to sacrifice Isaac, the son who is to be the progenitor of the nations. Isaac was spared and later married Rebekah, who gave birth to twin sons Jacob and Esau.

Jacob, the second born, bought his brother's birthright with a pot of stew ("a mess of pottage") and gained Esau's blessing from their father by deception. God renamed him Israel (meaning "God strives" or "one who strives with God") after Jacob wrestled with a "man" that tradition identifies as an angel. Israel's twelve sons were to be the forebears of the twelve tribes of Israel.[6] Esau's descendants, the Edomites, are to engage in ongoing rivalry with Israel throughout much of Edom's history.

Jacob's favorite son, Joseph, was sold to Egyptians by his brothers. When Jacob's family later was forced to migrate to Egypt during a famine, Joseph saved the family by providing them food. Jacob's descendants, the Israelites, were subsequently enslaved during their time in Egypt until freed by God in the Exodus.

Genesis was written when the Hebrew people continued to ask Who are we and how did we get here? The stories told in households and around campfires for centuries were gathered together and recorded in this book.

Outlines

Primeval history (chapters 1–11); Patriarchal history (12–50).

Creation (1–2); Adam and Eve (2–5); Noah (6–10); Abraham and Sarah (12–20); Isaac and Rebekah (21–26); Jacob and Rachel (27–36); Joseph (37–50).

[6]Israel is a name applied to the Hebrew people (Israelites) and country (Israel).

Famous Passages (Chapters and Verses)

First and second creation stories—1:1–2:4 and 2:4–3:24
God created humans in own image—1:27
Adam and Eve and the forbidden fruit—3
Cain kills Abel, asks, "Am I my brother's keeper?"—4:1–16
Noah and the flood—6–9
Noahaic covenant—9
Tower of Babel—11:1–9
Call of Abraham and Sarah—12:1–9
Covenant with Abraham—15 and 17
Hagar bears Abram a son, Ishmael—16
Circumcision as sign of covenant—17:9–14
Destruction of Sodom and Gomorrah—18 and 19
Sarah gives birth to Isaac—21:1–8
Hagar and Ishmael banished—21:9–21
Abraham's offering of Isaac—22:1–19
Isaac and Rebekah—24
Jacob and Esau's birthright—27–28
Jacob wrestles with angel, renamed Israel—32:22–32 (on Jacob's
    name, see also 35:1–15)
Jacob's son Joseph sold by brothers—37:1–36
Joseph and Potiphar's wife—39:1–23
Joseph interprets Pharaoh's dreams—40 and 41
Joseph gives food to his brothers—42–45
Joseph reunited with his father—46:28–48:22
Blessing of Jacob—49

⚜

EXODUS

NARRATIVE

This book picks up the story several hundred years after the close of Genesis, when the Israelites[7] living in Egypt (see Genesis 37–50) had multiplied and been enslaved. It tells how God called Moses to lead them out of slavery in Egypt, made a covenant with them, and gave them the Law (or instruction).

Initially the Pharaoh (king) of Egypt did not want to let the Israelites leave. But after ten plagues he relented. The final plague was the death of every firstborn son. The Israelites were instructed to prepare a lamb and mark their doorposts with its blood. This way God's angel would know to "pass over" their houses and spare their sons. They also were to stand ready to leave immediately. This event is recalled in the Passover service (which includes a meal of unleavened bread, bitter herbs, and lamb). Passover is observed by Jews today and is reflected in the story of Jesus and the Christian Eucharist.[8] The Exodus story is central to both the Jewish and Christian faiths.

When the Israelites left Egypt, pursued by the Pharaoh, they crossed the Red Sea (where the pursuing Egyptians were drowned). They then entered a long period of wilderness wandering. During that time Moses received the Sinai (also called the Mosaic) covenant, which described

---

[7]Israelites (the Hebrew people) are descendants of Israel, who was previously named Jacob (see Genesis 32:22–32). They are the ancestors of today's ethnic Jews (those born Jews rather than those who adopt the Jewish faith).

[8]The Eucharist is a worship service in which some Christian traditions memorialize Christ (recall what happened), and other traditions celebrate him as present in the consecrated bread and wine. This practice grows out of Jesus' observation of the traditional Jewish Passover meal. When praying the traditional blessings over bread and wine at his last Passover with his disciples, he identified those elements as his body and blood.

the promises of God, the behaviors expected by God, and the consequences of obedience and disobedience. The Israelites promptly broke the covenant by worshiping a golden calf, a clear instance of idolatry, but quickly repented. God responded by renewing the covenant and, through Moses, gave the people the Ten Commandments again. These ten laws (or instructions) give an overview of most of the laws given throughout the Hebrew Bible. Four of the ten relate to one's relationship with God, while six of them deal with justice and right behavior toward one's neighbor, the poor, and the oppressed. They demonstrate how people are to live in right relationship with God and each other.

Outlines

Oppression in Egypt, God's deliverance (1–18); terms of the covenant with God (19–40).

Israelites enslaved (1); Moses' birth/life (2–4); Moses confronts Pharaoh (5–6); the plagues (7–11); Passover and Exodus from Egypt (12–15); wandering in the wilderness (16–18); covenant at Mount Sinai given (19–31) followed by Israel's response (32–40).

Famous Passages

Moses' birth and his adoption by Pharaoh's daughter—2:1–10
Moses and the burning bush—3:2–6
God's name revealed: "I AM" 3:14
"I will free you . . . take you as my people and I will be your God"—6:6–7
Plagues in Egypt—7:14–11:10
Passover and escape from Egypt (Exodus)—12:1–13:16
Crossing the Red Sea—13:17–15:21
Moses and Miriam's song—15:1–21

Wandering in the wilderness—15:22–20:26; 31:18–34:35 (also
    Numbers 20–21)
Israelites fed with manna from God—16:2–36
Provision of water from rock at Meribah—17:1–7
Military victory while Moses' arms are raised—17:8–13
Moses selects others to share leadership—18:13–27
"If you . . . keep my covenant . . . you shall be my treasured
    possession . . . a holy nation"—19:5–6
Ten Commandments given on stone tablets—20:1–7 (cf. 31:18,
    34:12–26; also Deuteronomy 5:1–21)
Israelites make an idol calf of gold, covenant broken, tablets
    destroyed—32
Moses sees "God's back"—33:12–23
Covenant renewed; Ten Commandments given again—34
Ark of the Covenant—37:1–9
Tabernacle established—40

LEVITICUS

MANUAL OF RULES

More than any book in the Bible, Leviticus details regulations and instructions for Israelites. It guides
priests of the tribe of Levi (Levites) and lay people on
matters of worship, purity, and ritual. Because much of it
applies to priests, it is sometimes called the Priests' Manual. Though most of the laws are designed to apply to
everyone, the priests were responsible for teaching everyone the rules and ethical principles behind them. The
priest was to be the intermediary between God and the
individual or nation, using prayer and ritual actions to
intercede on their behalf.

Leviticus focuses on holiness and how an unholy people
can come into relationship with a holy God. The Day of
Atonement (today known as Yom Kippur and still observed

by Jews), was the day the high priest entered into the most holy part of the tabernacle (the Holy of Holies) to make atonement. The goal was "to cleanse [the people]; from all [their] sins [they] shall be clean before the Lord" (16:30).

The book outlines how people can maintain purity for themselves, their homes, foods, and relationships. For example, the scriptural basis for today's Jewish dietary laws (what is kosher, or ritually pure) is found here.

Outline

Instructions for worshipers regarding sacrifices and offerings (1–7); ordination of priests (8–10); uncleanness rituals and food instructions (11–15); Day of Atonement (16); Holiness Code (17–26); rules about religious vows (27).

Famous Passages

Prohibition against eating pork—11:7
Prohibition against eating blood—17:10–14
"Love your neighbor as yourself"—19:18
Sabbath day of rest—23:3
Jewish feasts of Unleavened Bread, Weeks, Trumpets, Atonement, and Booths—23
Sabbatical year; year of Jubilee—25

NUMBERS

NARRATIVE

Numbers tells the story of how the Israelites failed to believe God's promise and thus were consigned to wandering in the wilderness for forty years. Only the succeeding generation finally entered the Promised Land (Canaan).

The book begins and ends by giving long census reports; it also outlines the people's travels and gives more regulations. It describes the Israelites' complaining and faithlessness during their travels and shows that God still kept promises made. When they neared the Promised Land, Moses sent spies to observe and inspect it. On their return, the people became frightened by the spies' report of the inhabitants' strength. They refused to enter the land. So God decided to wait for the next generation to lead the invasion.

During the time covered in Numbers the focus of divine revelation shifts from the mountain (Sinai) to the Tent of Meeting, where rested the Ark (container) holding the tablets with the Ten Commandments. The Tent of Meeting was portable and could travel with them.

Outlines

In the wilderness of Sinai (1–10); journey through the wilderness to Transjordan (10–22); settlement in the plains of Moab (22–36).

First census (1); organization and preparation (2–5); sanctification and departure (6–10); complaints (11–12); spies sent into Canaan (13); the people rebel and Moses intercedes (14–15); revolt against Moses and Aaron (16–17) Miriam and Aaron die (20); people journey to Moab (21–25); second census (26); organization and regulations (27–30); preparation of next generation for conquest (31–36).

Famous Passages

Leaders selected to help Moses; Spirit also given to two who were not selected—11:16–30
Spies sent to Canaan—13 and 14

Complainers not to inhabit Canaan—14:22–23
Revolt against Moses; leaders swallowed by earth—16
Aaron's rod buds as a sign—17
Water flows from the rock at Meribah—20
Balaam stories (the talking donkey)—22–24
Joshua appointed Moses' successor—27:12–23

DEUTERONOMY

LAW AND NARRATIVE

Deuteronomy tells us that Moses was never allowed to enter Canaan, but he did see it from a mountaintop. This book presents a series of Moses' speeches that describe the behaviors God expects. They were meant to inspire the people to recommit themselves to the covenant with God. One reviewed the wilderness experience, another the laws of God, and a third addressed the renewal of the covenant. Throughout the book, instruction is intertwined with story and with a call to "remember" God's deeds.

This book is the last of the five books of the Pentateuch. Together with Joshua, Judges, 1 and 2 Samuel, and 1 and 2 Kings, it is part of the "Deuteronomic history," a narrative of events in Israel's wilderness period. It repeats much of the law found in the previous three books and its story is repeated in the books that follow it.

Deuteronomy contains the Shema (which means "Listen!") in 6:4–8. It is virtually a Jewish creed, part of which ("you shall love the Lord your God with all your heart . . . soul . . . might") was quoted by Jesus as "the greatest commandment."

Outlines

Moses' first discourse (1:6–4:40); second discourse (5:1–11:32); and third discourse (29:1–30:20).

Review of wilderness travels (1:4); review of the Sinai Covenant (5)
and implications of it (6–11); restatement of covenant
(12–26:15); ratification and reaffirmation of covenant
(26:16–28:68); covenant enacted in Moab (29–30); Joshua
commissioned (31); Moses' song (32), blessing (33), and
death (34).

Famous Passages

Ten Commandments—5:6–21
Love God with heart, soul, might (Shema); bind law on hand,
    forehead, doorposts—6:4–9
"Do not put the Lord your God to the test"—6:16
Promised Land described—8:7–10
"What does the Lord your God require of you?"—10:12–13
One sanctuary to worship God—12
Tithing rule—14:22–29
Forgiving debts (sabbatical year)—15
Two witnesses required to convict—19:15–20
"Eye for eye, tooth for tooth"—19:21
"This very day you have become the people of the Lord your God.
    Therefore obey . . . his commandments"—27:9–10
Commandment is not too difficult—30:11–14
"Choose life so that you . . . may live"—30:15–20
Song of Moses—32

THE PROPHETS

The Prophets section of the Hebrew Scriptures breaks down into two blocks of material: the Early Prophets and the Later Prophets. Whereas the Early Prophets section includes primarily historical books—Joshua, Judges, Samuel, and Kings—the books named after Israel's prophets (Isaiah, Jeremiah, Ezekiel, and the twelve minor prophets), which contain proclamations of God's word and predictions of future events, fall within the Later Prophets section. In addition, the Christian order of books inserts Ruth between Judges and Samuel, and separates the Early and Later Prophets sections—between Kings and Isaiah—with the Writings portion of Hebrew Scripture.

THE EARLY PROPHETS

The books classified in the Hebrew Bible as the Early Prophets contain the narrative history of Israel. Joshua, Judges, 1 and 2 Samuel, and 1 and 2 Kings tell the story of the former Hebrew slaves beginning with their arrival in the Promised Land. These books move from the conquest and settlement, through the establishment of a monarchy, through the heyday of David and Solomon, to the split of the northern tribes—Israel—from the southern tribes—Judah—and the eventual decline and fall of both kingdoms to invading foreign empires.

1,150 – 1,100	1,100 – 1,050	1,050 – 925	924 – 722	722 – 586
Conquest and Settlement	*Period of the Judges*	*Saul, David, Solomon*	*Divided Kingdom*	*The Fall of Judah*

❋❋❋❋
JOSHUA

NARRATIVE

Joshua succeeded Moses as the leader of the Israelites. This book is an account of the Hebrews' conquest of Canaan (the Promised Land) with Joshua leading the army. It presents the complicated and perhaps incomplete conquest as simple and decisive. For the modern reader the value of the book is as much theological as historical. Throughout the accounts the writer emphasizes God's ability to act in power and fulfill his promises.

The book opens with Joshua leading the people across the Jordan River into Canaan. They first conquered Jericho, which fell after they circled it for six days, carrying the Ark of the Covenant. Other conquests follow, as does a tedious section describing the division of the land among the tribes (13–20). The writer repeatedly stresses the need to eliminate other religious practices and to be devoted only to God. The book closes with Joshua's last words to the people. He reminds them that they were promised this land long ago and can claim it through their relationship with Abraham, but can enjoy it in peace only if they live in accordance with God's covenant.

Outline

Joshua appointed and spies sent to Jericho (1–2); Israelites cross Jordan, destroy Jericho (3–6), enter Promised Land, conquer south (7–10) and north (11); divide land among tribes (13–22); Joshua's farewell address (23), covenant at Shechem (24).

Famous Passages

The prostitute Rahab helps the Israelite spies sent into Canaan—2
Priests bearing Ark of the Covenant lead Israelites across Jordan River—3:14–17

Israelites circumcised to prepare for entry into Promised
    Land—5:2–9
March around and fall of Jericho—6
Sun stands still during battle—10:13–14
Cities of refuge for homicides—20

JUDGES

NARRATIVE

This book's title comes from the military and civic leaders who were "raised up" by God to deliver Israel from its oppressors. The judges were not arbiters of legal cases, as our modern use of the term would imply, as much as Spirit-endowed leaders and deliverers. The book chronicles battles following the conquest of Canaan that eventually put more land under Israelite control. It also outlines events related to each tribe.

Twelve judges are named, including Deborah, Gideon, and Samson. While the judges provided inspired leadership, the book also illustrates the moral decay that occurred among the people in the absence of godly leadership. The people themselves are often portrayed as disobedient, with corruption and violation of the law depicted as widespread at the end of the book. This set the stage for the rise of the monarchy (rule by kings).

The moral lesson of the book is that loyalty to God brings national blessing and success, while disloyalty guarantees disaster.

Outline

Tribes settle, become unfaithful (1–2); summary of judges: Ehud
    (3), Deborah (4–5), Gideon (6–9), Jephthah (10–12), Samson
    (13–16); story of the tribes of Dan and Benjamin (17–21).

Famous Passages

Ehud spears fat king—3:12–31
Jael drives a peg through Sisera's head—4:12–23
Deborah and Barak's song of victory—5
Gideon tests God with fleece—6:14–40
Gideon selects "water-lappers" to fight—7
Jephthah sacrifices his daughter—11:29–40
Samson and the Philistines—13
Delilah cuts Samson's hair—16

RUTH

NARRATIVE

This book recounts the touching, compelling story of Ruth, a Moabite woman, who after the death of her Judean husband left her homeland to go to Judah[9] with Naomi, her mother-in-law. She gleaned grain left for the poor after the harvest in the fields of Boaz, a distant relative of Naomi's, who befriended her. Naomi sent her to make herself available to Boaz, who took her as his wife. Ruth gave birth to Obed, who became the father of Jesse, who in turn became the father of King David, one of the most important persons in the Hebrew Bible. The story reminds us that David was part Moabite and therefore a "foreigner" whom God nevertheless used mightily. The book also shows Ruth's love and dedication and her important role in Hebrew history. Her pledge to Naomi (1:16–17) is often used in wedding services.

[9]After King Solomon's rule, the United Kingdom is divided into the Northern Kingdom (Israel) and the Southern Kingdom (Judah).

Outline

Ruth and Naomi leave Moab (1); Ruth gleans in Boaz's fields (2), approaches Boaz (3); Boaz settles next-of-kin rights (4:1–12), marries Ruth, who gives birth to Obed (4:13–17).

Famous Passages

"Where you go, I will go . . . your people shall be my people, and your God my God"—1:16–17

�֟ ✷ ✷

1 AND 2 SAMUEL

NARRATIVE

These books explain how and why kings came to reign over Israel and gives the account of Israel's first kings, Saul and David. The account begins with the elderly Eli, a high priest who served the temple with his corrupt sons. Into the temple came the childless Hannah, who prayed for a son and promised to dedicate him to God's service. Samuel was born as a result. He became a judge and prophet of Israel, and serves as the principal character in the first chapters of 1 Samuel.

The people asked Samuel to appoint a king for them so they could be like the other nations. God selected and Samuel anointed[10] Saul as the first king. We quickly learn about Saul's stellar successes and singular failures. Saul took over Samuel's role in offering sacrifice and thereby offended Samuel (and God). So Samuel anointed the boy

[10]Anointing here refers to a ceremonial appointment to office, usually using oil as a symbol.

David to succeed Saul. In a show of great faith and bravery, the young David killed the Philistine Goliath with a sling and five stones. He became a military hero beloved by the people and even Saul's son, Jonathan. But Saul quickly became jealous of him and eventually drove him into hiding.

The second book describes David's rule as king after Saul's death. Under his rule the nation was strong until he committed adultery, betrayal, and murder in the well-known account of his affair with Bathsheba. The closing years of David's life were filled with family problems: rape, murder, and insurrection.

In the Greek Bible this book, like 1 and 2 Kings, was a single work. As with all the Deuteronomic history books, it emphasizes fidelity to one God, worship at one sanctuary, and the election of the Israelites as God's chosen people through God's covenant.

Outlines

1 SAMUEL

Samuel born, left at the temple with the priest Eli (1–2), called by God (3); Philistines defeat Israel, take the Ark of the Covenant, God sends plagues (4–5); Philistines send the Ark back to Judah (6); Samuel leads as judge over Israel (7); Israel becomes a monarchy when Samuel anoints Saul as king (8–13); Saul is victorious over the Philistines (12–14) but is indicted for his disobedience and rejected as king (15). David is secretly anointed (16:1–13), slays the giant Goliath with a sling (17), and is an attendant in Saul's court until Saul threatens to kill him (18–20); David becomes an outlaw captain (21–26), seeks protection under the Philistines (27–29), and attacks the Amalekites (30) when Saul dies (31).

2 SAMUEL

David takes over as king of Judah (1), then Israel (2–5), brings the Ark to Jerusalem (6), and establishes the house of David (7).

He engages in war (8–10) and adultery (11–12). His daughter Tamar is raped by her half brother Amnon (13), who is killed by her brother Absalom (13–14). Absalom tries to take kingship from David and dies (15–19). The book ends with stories of insurrection and war (20–21), along with David's songs (22), last words (23), census decree, and building of an altar (24).

Famous Passages

1 SAMUEL

Birth and dedication of Samuel—1:1–28
Song of Hannah—2:1–10
Samuel's call and the priest Eli's counsel—3
Israel demands a king—8:1–22
Saul anointed and proclaimed king—9:1–10:24
Saul's unlawful sacrifice angers Samuel—13:1–14
Saul rejected by God—15:10–31
David anointed by Samuel—16:1–13
David and Goliath—17
David and Jonathan—19–20
David spares Saul's life—24:1–22

2 SAMUEL

David anointed king of Judah—2:1–7
David anointed king of Israel—5:1–5
Jerusalem becomes capital—5:6–10
Ark comes to Jerusalem—6:1–19
Nathan's oracle about David—7:12–13
David cares for Jonathan's son—9:1–13
David's adultery with Bathsheba and betrayal of Uriah—11:2–27
Nathan's parable of the lamb—12:1–15
David and Bathsheba's son dies—12:15–23
Rape of Tamar—13
Absalom's long hair hangs him—18:9–17
David's song: ''The Lord is my rock . . . in whom I take refuge''—22:2–51

❖ ❖ ❖

1 AND 2 KINGS

NARRATIVE

These books pick up where the books of Samuel left off; they recount David's death, Solomon's reign, and the accession of later kings. The underlying thesis is that the nation's future is determined by obedience to God's commandments. They include the sad record of various violations by kings and people alike.

The first book begins with Solomon assuming what will be his forty-year reign. Since it was a time of peace and prosperity, Solomon was able to build the temple planned by his father. Solomon was known for his wisdom, wealth, many wives, and the splendid temple he built. He was also known for the enslavement of his own people, his cruel treatment of others, and his corruption through the pagan influences of his foreign wives.

When Solomon's son Rehoboam took over after Solomon's death, the northern tribes of Israel asked him to lighten the people's oppressive tax burden. After consulting with his advisers, the king increased their burden instead. The tribes that had settled in the north rebelled, refused to accept him as king, and divided the kingdom (see map, page 308). They established Israel (the northern kingdom) as a separate nation with Jeroboam as their king. Israel was conquered by Assyria about 722 BCE. Judah (the southern kingdom) was conquered by Babylon in 597 and again in 587 BCE. Many residents were deported to Babylon. The end of the first book and all of the second book tell the stories of the two kingdoms along with their kings and prophets (such as Elijah and Elisha).

Outlines

1 KINGS

Solomon becomes king (1–2) and builds temple (4–7); temple dedicated (8); the reign of Solomon (9–11); Israel is divided and a succession of kings rule (12–16:28); Ahab and the prophet Elijah have a showdown (16:29–22:53).

2 KINGS

The prophet Elisha succeeds Elijah, performing miracles (1–8:6) and continuing to preach to the house of Ahab (8:7–10:31); kings of Israel and Judah reign (10:32–15:38); the northern kingdom (Israel) falls (16–17); Judah under Hezekiah (18–20) and Manasseh (21); Josiah reforms Judah (22–23:30); southern kingdom (Judah) falls (23:31–25:30).

Famous Passages

1 KINGS

Solomon's prayer for wisdom—3:3–14
Solomon's wisdom: ''Divide the living boy in two''—3:16–28
Temple and palace described—5:1–7:51
God's promise to Solomon—9:4–5
Queen of Sheba visits—10:1–13
Solomon's many wives, foreign gods—11:1–8
God's response to Solomon's sin—11:9–13
Rehoboam threatens heavier burdens, is rejected, sees kingdom divided—12:1–20
Elijah fed by ravens through drought—17:1–6
Elijah and widow's unending flour and oil—17:7–16
Elijah heals widow's son—17:17–23
Elijah's contest with priests of Baal—18:1–40
God's still, small voice (''a sound of sheer silence'')—19:9–15
Elijah calls Elisha—19:15–21
Jezebel kills Naboth to get vineyard for Ahab—21:1–29

2 KINGS

Elijah calls fire down on warriors—1:1–16
Elijah taken to heaven in whirlwind—2:1–12
Elisha receives Elijah's mantle—2:13–14
Elisha heals Naaman of leprosy—5
Elisha makes ax head float—6:1–7
Jehu executes Jezebel and royal family—9:1–37
Assyria conquers Israel—17:21–23
Eight-year-old Josiah becomes king—22:1–2
Josiah's reforms—23:1–25
God rejects Judah—23:27
Judah, Jerusalem conquered—25:8–11

THE WRITINGS

In Hebrew Scriptures the Writings portion is the final third. The books in this section of the Bible represent a catchall of literature ranging from books of poetry, love songs, proverbs, and wisdom sayings to short stories, novellas, and narrative history. Christian Bibles present the Writings as a block of material between the Early and Later Prophets sections, with the exception of Ruth, which falls between Judges and Samuel.

꙳ ꙳ ꙳ ꙳

1 AND 2 CHRONICLES

NARRATIVE

The Chronicles represent a sort of condensed version of Samuel–Kings, repeating and recasting much of the same material. The books thereby provide a second history of the glorious days of David and Solomon. Some scholars believe that at one point the Chronicler's work included Ezra and Nehemiah (which have the same style and theological point of view) in one book.

The Chronicler writes from a priestly perspective; he may have been a Levite or other member of the temple

1,025 – 586	586 – 500	500 – 332	332 – 250	250 – 150
Israelite Kingdom	Period of Exile	Jews Return from Exile	Rise of Hellenism	Jews under Hellenism

staff. Sometimes he excerpts passages word for word from Samuel–Kings. Other times he reinterprets events to make clear his conviction that Israel was called to be a worshiping community, a holy nation whose whole life was to be lived in service to God.

The first nine chapters of the first book contain genealogies. The tenth chapter begins the story of David and focuses on the Ark of the Covenant, how it was set up, how worship and proper service at the temple were established, and who were the people responsible for leading it. Where Samuel–Kings portrays David as a political leader, the Chronicler emphasizes David's importance in organizing Israel as a worshiping community. Because he does not want to detract from David's role as a religious leader, he ignores David's outlaw activities, adultery, and his deathbed orders to kill Joab and Shimei. Instead, he focuses on David's work in establishing religion and his deathbed vision of the future temple.

The second book begins with Solomon; the first nine chapters repeat the stories about his reign. The rest of the book is about Judah, the southern kingdom. It shows that proper worship was led by priests descended from the tribe of Levi and Aaron who served at the temple in the time of David. And it shows that proper kingly rule was led by kings descended from David. The Chronicler likes to stress that Judah was ruled by the descendants of David and could thus lay claim to true worship and kingship, unlike Israel, the kingdom in the north.

Outlines

1 CHRONICLES

Genealogies from Adam to Saul (1–9); David succeeds Saul as king (10–16), plans temple (17), goes to war (18), takes a census (21), and prepares to build the temple (22–28); Solomon succeeds David as king (29).

2 CHRONICLES

Solomon's reign (1–9); kings of Judah (10–28); Hezekiah and his
successors (29–33); Josiah's reforms (34–35); the last kings of
Judah (36).

Famous Passages

1 CHRONICLES

King Saul's suicide—10:1–14
David anointed king—11:1–3
Jerusalem established as City of David—11:4–7
Ark brought to Jerusalem and set up under tent—15:1–16:6
God's covenant with David—17:1–15
David's prayer of blessing—29:10–19

2 CHRONICLES

Solomon asks for wisdom—1:7–13
Temple built—3:1
Ark brought from tent to temple—5:2–14
Temple dedicated—6:1–7:3
God's covenant with Solomon—7:17–20
Queen of Sheba visits—9:1–12
Egypt attacks Judah, ransacks temple—12:1–10
Hezekiah restores temple worship—29:1–36
Great Passover in Jerusalem—30:1–27
Eight-year-old Josiah reigns—34:1–7
Book of the Law discovered, read—34:8–30
Covenant renewed—34:31–33
Fall of Jerusalem; people exiled to Babylon—36:15–21
King Cyrus of Persia announces liberty for the exiles—36:22–23

EZRA

NARRATIVE

When the Israelites of the northern kingdom and later the people of Judah were exiled to Babylonia, they had to find new ways to worship. Sometimes called the "Jews of the Diaspora,"[11] they gathered in groups which became synagogues (meaning assemblies) to study the law and encourage one another. When the political winds changed and Persia became the leading power, a remnant returned to the land of Israel.

The book of Ezra relates stories of the return of the remaining Jews to Jerusalem after their exile. Ezra was a priest who urged people to follow God's law and rebuild Jerusalem and the temple. The book also includes a census and details about temple worship and responsibilities.

Many scholars believe this book was once part of a single work that included Chronicles and Nehemiah. The Chronicler's purpose was to strengthen the identity of the Israelites as a religious community. Because the Jewish people failed to worship God faithfully, the Chronicler believed, the temple was destroyed and they were taken captive. He portrayed the people returning from exile not so much as a nation but as a religious community. Ezra brought the law of Moses and instituted a religious reform that would reestablish the community's holiness.

Outline

Exiles return to Jerusalem with Sheshbazzar (1–2), restore temple (3–6); Ezra's instructions to the returning exiles (7–10).

[11]The word *Jew* comes from *Judah* and refers here to descendants of Abraham. In earlier books the same people are called "the Hebrew people" or "Israelites." *Diaspora* means dispersion or scattering.

Famous Passages

King Cyrus of Persia decrees rebuilding of temple—1:2–4
King Artaxerxes issues decree to stop building—4:1–24
King Darius mandates resumption of work—5:1–6:12
Temple completed—6:13–15
Ezra returns to Jerusalem to lead—7:6, 9–10
Foreign wives and children rejected—10:1–17, 44

NEHEMIAH

NARRATIVE

Nehemiah, a Jewish official who reported to King Artaxerxes, was appointed governor of Judea. This book contains his personal reflections on life after the exile and his leadership as he worked with Ezra to finish the temple and restore religious fervor (see the Book of Ezra).

Nehemiah lived in Persia and made two trips to Jerusalem, one in 445/444 BCE for twelve years and the second sometime later. Nehemiah initially organized people to rebuild the city walls in fifty-five days so they could be more secure. As governor he led the people, upheld the law, and dealt with allies and enemies among the surrounding nations.

Outline

Nehemiah's commission (1–2:10); Jerusalem rebuild (2–4); social reforms (5–7), covenant and its obligations renewed (8–12); religious reforms (13).

Famous Passages

Abolition of pledges for debt—5:1–13
Law read in front of Water Gate—8:1–18

National confession—9:1–37
Covenant renewed—10:28–39

ESTHER

NARRATIVE

The book of Esther tells of a Jewish girl who became queen of Persia when her predecessor refused the king's command to show her beauty to his drunken party companions. During Esther's reign a young court official, Haman gains increased power. When he is unable to get the Jews, especially Mordecai, to bow and do obeisance to him, he connives to annihilate all Jews, not realizing that the queen is Jewish and that Mordecai is her cousin. At great risk to herself, Esther gains the king's favor and exposes the plot. Haman is hanged in the gallows he designed for Mordecai and Mordecai assumes the vacated office. The feast of Purim was inaugurated to commemorate this compelling story.

Outline

King Ahasuerus removes Vashti as queen (1), installs Esther (2); Haman's plot (3); Esther plans rescue (4) and tells king about plot (5); Haman is executed (6–8); Jews destroy enemies (8–9:19) and celebrate feast of Purim (9:20–10:3).

Famous Passages

Queen Vashti rebels, is deposed—1:10–22
''If you keep silence at such a time as this . . .''—4:14
Feast of Purim—9:1–32

JOB

POETIC STORY

This book explores why "bad things happen to good people." It is a theological exploration of the problem of how a just God can allow the innocent to suffer. It does not provide easy answers, but engages the reader in wrestling with the questions.

The book is written like a play. After introducing Job, a successful farmer with ten children, the book describes a conversation between God and Satan. Satan argued that Job worshiped God only because he was successful. Satan challenged God to see what would happen if Job experienced misfortune. Job immediately encountered a host of troubles that left him poor, childless, and badly diseased. Still Job worshiped God. Job's "friends" came to comfort him and convince him that he must have sinned to reap such punishment from God. But Job argued that he did nothing wrong.

Finally Job asked God, "Why?" God answered "out of the whirlwind," chiding Job for questioning him, and reassuring Job that God has been and will always be present. Job then reaffirmed his trust in God and said that he was sorry he ever said anything in the first place! God defended Job to his friends, and Job prayed for his friends. The book ends with God restoring all of Job's good fortune, including another ten children.

While biblical material before this often stresses that God rewards goodness and punishes evil, the writer of Job maintains that the good person who suffers is not being punished by God and in fact remains in God's presence. Good people sometimes suffer for reasons that are not evident or understandable. Job provides a model of faithfulness, no matter what happens.

Outline

Introduction, a meeting between God and "heavenly beings"
(1–2); Job's complaint (3); three speeches between Job and
his friends in the form of poems (4–14, 15–21, 22–26); God's
wisdom (28); Job's summary (29–31); Elihu's speech (32–37);
God's answer and Job's response (38–42:6); epilogue
(42:7–17).

Famous Passages

"Naked I came from my mother's womb, and naked I shall return
there."—1:21
"The Lord gave, and the Lord has taken away."—1:21
"I know that my Redeemer lives—"19:25
Where wisdom is to be found—28
God's answer to Job—38–41
"Who is this that darkens counsel by words without
knowledge?"—38:2
"Where were you when I laid the foundation of the earth?"—38:4
"I know that you can do all things. . . . I have uttered what I did
not understand"—42:2–3

✤ ✤

PSALMS

POEMS/HYMNS

Called by some the "prayer book of the Bible," the
Psalms gather a rich collection of 150 prayers, poems,
and hymns of various types. These include laments (for
times of trouble), thanksgiving (for God's action), hymns
(to praise God), enthronement hymns (to celebrate God's
kingship), royal Psalms (about the nation's kings), wisdom Psalms (insights from wise teachers), prophetic judg-
ments, vows, worship Psalms, and benedictions. Much of

the material probably served as a hymnal and prayer book for temple worship in Jerusalem. Words scattered throughout some Psalms (such as *selah*) appear to be directions to the chanters.

The Psalms express a wide range of emotions: anger, joy, grief, awe, gratitude, and pleas for help or protection. Many people memorize favorite Psalms; their poetic structure makes them easy to remember.

Outline

The Psalms are divided into five books—I (1–41), II (42–72), III (73–89), IV (90–106), V (107–150).

Famous Passages

"Happy are those who do not follow the advice of the wicked."—1:1–6

"Let the words of my mouth and the meditation of my heart be acceptable to you."—19:14

"My God . . . why have you forsaken me?"—22:1–31

"The Lord is my shepherd."—23:1–6

"Who shall ascend the hill of the Lord?"—24:3–6

"The Lord is my light and my salvation."—27:1–14

"In you, O Lord, I seek refuge."—31:1–24

"Happy are those whose transgression is forgiven."—32:1–11

"Trust in the Lord. . . . Take delight in the Lord, and he will give you the desires of your heart."—37:3–11

"O Lord, do not rebuke me in anger."—38:1–22

"As a deer longs for flowing streams, so my soul longs for you."—42:1–11

"God is our refuge and strength, a very present help."—46:1–3

"Be still, and know that I am God!"—46:10

"Have mercy on me, O God. . . . Create in me a clean heart."—51:1:17

"For God alone my soul waits in silence."—62:1–12

"God, you are my God; I seek you, my soul thirsts for
    you."—63:1–4

"May God be gracious to us and bless us."—67:1–7

"Save me, O God, for the waters have come up to my
    neck."—69:1–33

"He delivers the needy . . . poor . . . weak."—72:12–14

"Happy are those who live in your house . . . a day in your courts
    is better than a thousand elsewhere."—84:1–12

"You who live in shelter of the Most High."—91:1–16

"O come, let us sing to the Lord."—95:1–7

"It is [God] that made us . . . we are his people, the sheep of his
    pasture."—100:1–5

"Bless the Lord, O my soul."—103:1–18

"I will lift up my eyes to the hills—from where will my help
    come?"—121:1–8

"By the rivers of Babylon—there we sat down and . . . wept . . .
    we hung up our harps. . . . How could we sing . . . in a foreign
    land?"—137:1–9

✤ ✤ ✤ ✤
PROVERBS

SAYINGS

Proverbs offers practical guidance for the person who
wants to know and follow God. Designed for instruction in home, temple court, and school, the book gathers
wise sayings and commonsense teachings on how to live
a godly life. The compilers drew some of the sayings from
other Middle Eastern religious traditions or even secular
life, but included them because all insight was seen as a
gift of God. This book is best read by dipping into individual sayings rather than reading the whole volume—there
are hundreds of proverbs arranged in no particular order.

Outline

Collection of the more religious sayings (1–9); collection of one-line secular sayings (10:1–22:16); thirty Egyptian wise sayings (22:17–24:22 or 34); more secular sayings (25–29); appendixes (30–31).

Famous Passages

The fear of the Lord is the beginning of knowledge—1:7
Trust in the Lord; do not rely on your own insight—3:5–8
Go to the ant, you sluggard, observe—6:6–11
A mild answer turns away anger—15:1
Pride goes before a fall—16:18
Start child on the right road . . . will not leave it—22:6

✳ ✳ ✳ ✳
ECCLESIASTES

WISDOM LITERATURE

Unique in style and theology, this book says that God is largely incomprehensible and life is full of futility. It seeks to show that all goals result in disappointment and frustration if they are pursued apart from God and as mere ends in themselves. Even life at its best, says the writer, is troubled by injustice and death. Because of the writer's focus on life's limits and absurd moments, vanity (or emptiness) is a key word. Nevertheless, Ecclesiastes repeatedly urges humans to "fear [i.e. hold in awe and reverence] God, and keep his commandments" and to embrace life and its gifts.

The book raises many questions still asked today. Gloomy, sometimes cynical, it concludes that despite all, worshiping God and keeping God's laws is the best course of action. This is a good book for those who find the Bible "out of touch with real life" as it expresses many basic human feelings.

Outline

Futility of all labors (1–6); wisdom and folly (7–11); advice to a
   young man (12).

Famous Passages

All is vanity; everything is futile—1:2
Eat, drink, and be merry—2:24–25
For everything there is a season, a time to . . .—3:1–8
Toil produces nothing you can take with you—5:15
Fear God, keep commandments; that is the whole duty of
   everyone—12:13–14

THE SONG OF SOLOMON

LOVE SONGS

This collection of songs describes and upholds deep, passionate love between a man and a woman, contrasting it with transient love. It describes seduction, surrender, joy at union, and marriage. Unique in the Bible, it is sometimes used with premarital counseling or at weddings. The Song of Solomon (also known as the Song of Songs) has often been seen as an allegory for God's love of people. For Christians, it has been seen as an allegory of Christ's love for the church.

Outline

Opening songs (1:1–2:7); spring seen as season is for love
   (2:8–17); separation, reunion (3:1–5); wedding procession
   (3:6–11); lover describes his beloved (4); dream song (5:1–8);
   lover describes her beloved (5:9–7:9); love fulfilled (7:10–8:4);
   love's power (8:6–7); little sister (8:8–12).

Famous Passages

I am dark and lovely—1:6
I am my beloved's, his desire is for me—7:10
Love is strong as death—8:6
Many waters cannot quench love—8:7

THE LATER PROPHETS

With the books known as the Later Prophets, we meet the
colorful and charismatic spokespersons of God. The
major prophets are famous people with long books—
Isaiah, Jeremiah, and Ezekiel—while the twelve minor
prophets vary in their notoriety and the length of their
writings. In the Christian Bible Daniel follows Ezekiel as
a prophetic book, but in the Hebrew Bible it is grouped
with the writings.

843 – 745	744 – 640	639 – 586	586 – 500	500 – 332
Jehu Dynasty	Period of Assyrian Domination	Fall of Judah to Babylon	Period of Exile	Jews Return from Exile

❖ ❖

ISAIAH

PROPHECY

I saiah begins a series of books by prophets—people who spoke the word of God as it was given to them. Some of the prophets spoke only once or twice, some became prominent leaders. Succession was by God's call, not by birth (as was the case with kings and priests).

Isaiah is made up of three collections of literature (prose and poetry) by two or three writers from different periods of history. In the first section (chapters 1–39) the prophet Isaiah (c. 742–701 BCE) calls people to trust God, not governments. The second section (40–55), written near the end of the Exile (587–539 BCE), encourages those about to return to Jerusalem. The third section (56–66), written during the postexilic period, encourages those reestablishing life in the Promised Land.

Important themes include God's sovereignty, God's plans to save the people who look to him, the Messiah's coming, and the importance of social justice. Significant portions of Handel's *Messiah* are based on passages from this book (see 35, 40, 52, 53). In Luke 4, Jesus identified himself with Chapter 61 and much of the imagery the church employs for Jesus comes from this book.

Outline

lament and God's response (63–64); judgment and salvation (65–66).

Famous Passages

Beat swords into plowshares, spears . . .—2:4
Isaiah's call; burning coal touches lips—6
People that walked in darkness, seen light—9:2
For to us a child is born, son given—9:6–7
With justice he will judge the poor—11:1–5
Wolf will live with the lamb—11:6–9
Let the wilderness be glad . . . water will spring up . . . a highway
    will appear . . .—35
Prepare a highway . . . for our God—40:1–11
Here is my servant . . . my chosen one—42:1–9
How beautiful . . . are the feet of the herald—52:7–10
He was despised . . . bore our pain . . . by his wounds we are
    healed . . . 53:2–6
All we like sheep have gone astray—53:6
Seek the Lord while he may be found . . . for my thoughts are not
    your thoughts—55:6–11
Arise, shine . . . your light has come—60:1–3, 19–20
The spirit of the Lord . . . has sent me to announce good news to
    the poor . . . liberty to captives—61:1–3

JEREMIAH

PROPHECY

After King Josiah's religious reforms, the people believed that they would soon return to the glorious days of King David. They were confident in understanding themselves as God's chosen people. They believed in God's continual presence in the temple. But the prophet Jeremiah shocked them by preaching that God's presence and their role as the people of God was dependent on their faithfulness. He denounced their outward "show" of religion while their inward hearts were hardened. People were putting their trust in religious institutions (the Ark, the Law, the sacrifices, the temple) while exhibiting treachery among themselves and unfaithfulness to God.

Jeremiah writes about the coming destruction of Jerusalem and the temple. Because of the painfulness of the situation, Jeremiah is sometimes called the "weeping prophet." He also described what happened during the last days of the kingdom. He believed that only through the pain of this crisis would people return to true relationships with God and one another. He also provided comfort by trying to convince the people that they could survive without the temple.

Jeremiah is more an anthology than a story. The first twenty-five chapters give his oracles[12] with a few biographical notes. Chapters 26–45 are largely biographical with an occasional sermon added. The last block of material contains oracles against other nations, probably gathered from various sources.

Outline

Jeremiah's call (1); the prophet's appeal for repentance (2–6); consequences of false religion (7–10); covenant broken (11); judgment (12–17); images of potter and clay and broken jug (18–20); biography of Jeremiah's ministry (21–45) with key promises (30–31); prophecies against foreign nations (46–51); destruction of Jerusalem (52).

Famous Passages

Before I formed you in the womb I knew you . . . consecrated you—1:5

---

[12]Communications from God. The word also may convey the idea of a "burden" or saying.

Blessed . . . who trusts in the Lord . . . will be like a tree planted by the waterside—17:5–8

Potter and clay story—18:1–11

Establish a new covenant; set my law in their hearts; I shall be their God—31:31–34

Jeremiah's scroll read, burned—36:1–32

LAMENTATIONS

POEMS

Five poems mourn the loss of the temple and Jerusalem to Babylonian conquerors. The first four poems are alphabetic acrostics. The poems use three voices: one commenting on Jerusalem, one speaking as the city itself, and the third voicing hope. These passages are sometimes used for mourning in worship or to help people express grief. They are often used in Christian liturgies during Holy Week.

Outline

Sorrows of the captive Zion (Jerusalem) (1); God's anger (2); Zion's hope after punishment (3–4); prayer for remembrance and restoration (5).

Famous Passages

Friends have betrayed . . . become enemies—1:2

Love of the Lord never ceases, mercy never ends—3:22–25

Examine our ways . . . turn back to the Lord—3:40

Lord was in the right for I rebelled against his command—1:18

Lord's love is not exhausted, nor has his compassion failed—3:22–33

EZEKIEL

PROPHECY

Ezekiel, a prophet and priest, lived during the last years of the kingdom of Judah and the Babylonian captivity following the destruction of the temple. He was one of the people exiled during the years before Jerusalem finally fell to Babylon.

During this time the Jewish religion saw significant transitions. It moved from being a religion identified with a land and temple to one identified with people, the synagogue, and the study of the Law—the essential components of Judaism today.

Ezekiel begins by talking about the problems that caused the defeat of Israel, urging them to learn from their mistakes and to live under the Law, even though they were in a foreign land. Toward the end of the book he paints a vision of the glorious temple and joyous times that would come in the future—a vision to give people hope as they lived under the oppressive rule of their conquerors.

Ezekiel acted out his prophecies in rather bizarre dramas such as being bound in ropes and lying on his left side 390 days and then his right for forty days. This enactment was to signify Israel and Judah's coming punishment (4:1–8). Shaving his head and beard, burning the hair, and scattering it around the city (5:1–4) was designed to make a similar point.

Ezekiel saw God as beyond human comprehension—a God who, for the sake of God's "holy name" forgives people and puts a new "spirit" within them. Previously God had been seen as punishing wrongdoing and requiring repentance as a costly condition of forgiveness and restoration. Ezekiel envisioned punishment as a consequence of wrongdoing, forgiveness as freely given, and thus repentance available as a choice. He stressed people's freedom of choice and responsibility.

Outline

Call of Ezekiel and vision of chariot (1–3); prophecies about the coming destruction of Jerusalem (4–5); God's judgment (6–11); Judah's fate predicted (12–24); prophecies against enemy nations (25–32); Ezekiel prepares for the restored kingdom (33–39); the new temple (40–47:12); division of land among the tribes (47:13–48:35).

Famous Passages

Vision of wheels within wheels—1:4–28; 10:1–22
God forgives, loves like faithful spouse—16
Parents eat sour grapes, children's teeth set on edge; person who sins will suffer consequence—18:2–32
God is the true shepherd—34:11–31
I will put a new "spirit" within you; remove heart of stone, give you heart of flesh—36:22–28
Valley of dry bones—37:1–14

DANIEL

APOCALYPTIC LITERATURE

The book of Daniel is written in a form of writing known as *apocalyptic*, from a Greek word that means "disclose," "reveal," or "uncover"; the word usually refers to the "end times." Apocalyptic writing conveys a message (sometimes in coded language) received by someone from an otherworldly being. Daniel was written to encourage Jews facing persecution to remain faithful; its message was "keep the faith and God will come through for you."

The story began when Daniel, a young Jew exiled in Babylon, was assigned to serve in King Nebuchadnezzar's court. He interpreted the king's dreams and was given rewards and a position of authority. When the king required everyone to bow to a gold image, three young Jewish men refused to do so, were thrown into a furnace, but did not die. King Nebuchadnezzar immediately issued a decree honoring the God of Shadrach, Meshach, and Abednego, who was Daniel's God.

The king's next dream, which Daniel interpreted, foreshadowed the king's loss of kingly power and his descent into madness. His sanity was restored, however, and his kingdom and power returned, for which he praised Daniel's God. Daniel then interpreted the writing on a wall at a banquet given by King Nebuchadnezzar's son. Again he was rewarded. But when King Darius decreed that no one was to pray to anyone but the king, Daniel refused and was thrown into a den of lions. Through supernatural intervention he remained untouched.

The last vision in the book concerns the end of history. It was designed to encourage the Hebrew people by promising that God would ultimately vindicate the righteous.

Outline

Daniel and the three men selected and trained (1); Daniel interprets the king's vision (2); the golden image, three men in furnace (3); vision of the great tree; prediction that king would live like a wild beast (4); writing on the wall interpreted (5); Daniel in lion pit (6); Daniel's vision of four beasts and heaven (7–9); visions of conflict and struggle (10–12); prophetic glimpse of the end of time (12).

Famous Passages

Daniel's prayer of thanks for wisdom—2:20–23
Shadrach, Meshach, and Abednego in furnace—3:1–30
Nebuchadnezzar goes mad—4:28–33
Writing on the wall—5:5–9

Daniel in the lion pit—6:1–24
Michael will appear . . . and those whose name is entered into the
    book will awake—12:1–3

HOSEA

PROPHECY

I n the Hebrew Bible the minor prophets (those books
shorter than the major prophets) are called the Book of
the Twelve and are a literary unit arranged in what the
canonical compilers thought was chronological order (see
list on page 16).

Hosea is a prophet of the northern kingdom (Israel).
The book is an anthology of unrelated but moving poems
and prose. They present a startling shift of tone. Hosea
shows God as sharing in human feelings and agonies and
uses marriage imagery to make its points. God is portrayed as a faithful, forgiving husband, Israel as a wife who
is an adulterous "harlot." Hosea underscores the analogy
by acting it out in his own life, marrying a prostitute.

Outline

Unfaithful wife and Israel (1–3); God's indictment of Israel (4–9);
    God's judgment (10–13); the people's repentance and
    forgiveness (14).

Famous Passages

Hosea marries Gomer—1:2–7
Broken covenant; kill, rob, adultery, violence—4:1–4
My people turn away, but how can I give you up—11:7–9
Righteous walk in Lord's ways; sinners stumble—14:9

JOEL

APOCALYPTIC PROPHECY

The dramatic poetry of this visionary prophet focuses on God's victory over all—"the day of the Lord." This refers to a time of judgment when the wicked face destruction and the humble and oppressed are lifted up and delivered. Joel sees "the day of the Lord" as applying to Israel as well as to other nations. He uses distressing metaphors of locust plagues, ruinous destruction, and cosmic omens to convey the force of this coming time. The message is that Israel must repent and return to the Lord.

Outline

Locust plagues, repent (1); the day of the Lord is near, repent; God forgives (2); Judah's oppressors are punished and God reestablishes paradise (3).

Famous Passages

Rend your hearts, not garments; turn back to God . . . gracious and compassionate—2:13

I will pour out my spirit . . . sons and daughters will prophesy . . . dream dreams . . . see visions—2:28–29

Beat swords into pruning hooks—3:10

AMOS

PROPHECY

A mos is a short book that provides a good introduction to prophetic literature—a sort of "condensed version" of the other prophets. It is a compilation of speeches, hymns, visions, and other common prophetic elements.

Amos was a shepherd who lived about the same time as Hosea and Joel. He left his flocks to carry stern warnings about social and moral corruption to the nation's leaders, whom he held especially accountable. At a time of prosperity for the few—at the expense of the many—Amos issued uncompromising calls for justice and repentance. The leaders and their people would suffer punishment for their social injustice and religious arrogance. Because of this, Amos is often useful to those exploring issues of social justice.

Outline

Sins of Israel and neighbors (1–2); threatened punishments (3–6); visions of judgment (7–9:8); remnant spared; kingdom restored (9).

Famous Passages

They sell . . . the needy for a pair of shoes—2:6
Listen . . . you Bashan cows . . . who oppress the helpless and grind down the poor; you will be thrown on a dunghill—4:1
You that turn justice to poison—5:7
You that hate a man who brings a wrongdoer to court—5:10
Because you levy taxes on the poor . . . you built houses . . . will not live in them—5:11–13
Seek good, and not evil, that you may live—5:14

Establish justice in the courts—5:15
Let justice roll down like waters—5:23–24
Plumb-line set in the midst of God's people—7:7–9
I will send a famine of hearing the words of the Lord; they will
    seek, not find—8:11–12

OBADIAH

PROPHECY

This book of short poems from various sources is only twenty-one verses long. We know nothing about Obadiah, to whom the book is ascribed. But the poems predict that the neighboring nation of Edom would be punished for their pride and arrogance. The Edomites helped the Babylonians capture Jerusalem and they moved into the conquered territory. Traditionally Edomites have been identified as descendants of Esau, the twin of Jacob who was renamed Israel (see Genesis 25:24–34) and were long-standing enemies of Israel.

Obadiah, like Joel, talks about the coming day of the Lord, when all nations will be called to account for their actions. He discourages gloating over others' misfortunes because "as you have done, it will be done to you."

Outline

Edom's pride and downfall (1–14); their punishment and Israel's
    triumph over them (15–21).

Famous Passages

Though you soar as high as an eagle . . . even from there I shall
    bring you down—4

Do not gloat . . . when disaster strikes—12
You will be treated as you treat others—15

JONAH

STORY

A short story (or extended parable) about a man swallowed by a large fish when he refuses God's call to preach to the residents of Nineveh. Jonah finally did go to Nineveh, preached a one-verse message, and witnessed the people repent. Rather than rejoicing at the response, Jonah became angry when God forgave the people and did not carry out the predicted punishment. Jonah cannot believe that God cares for anyone or anything other than an Israelite.

The book conveys God's forgiving love for all. It countered the emerging attitude that said "God loves only us" by portraying the Jews' enemies as capable of repentance and loved by God. Jonah is sometimes used to explore human resistance to responding to God's call. God's question to Jonah at the end (4:9–11) invites the reader to apply and explore the issues personally.

Outline

Jonah avoids God's call to Nineveh, flees on a ship, storm arises; (1); Jonah thrown overboard and swallowed by whale (2); goes to Nineveh, preaches, they repent, God forgives (3); Jonah is resentful (4).

Famous Passages

Jonah's prayer in the belly of the ''whale''—2:1–9
Jonah's anger when God forgives—4:1–4

Gourd shelters Jonah, withers and dies . . . Jonah: "It is better for
me to die than to live"—4:6–11

MICAH

PROPHECY

A s with many of the prophets, Micah paints a picture of
God's constancy and mercy in the face of the people's
chronic idolatry. But he seemed concerned primarily with
ethical issues. He warned that the sins of Judah would
lead to God's punishment, with Assyria acting as God's
instrument of chastening. Micah focused on the behavior
of the nation's leaders, whom Micah sees as exploiting the
people. He spoke out against injustice and in defense of
the poor. The book moves between judgment and hope as
it shows God's faithfulness to the people.

Outline

Corrupt rulers and social evils denounced (1–3); God's people to
be restored (4–5); God's case against the people (6); call for
repentance and laying out of hope for restoration (7).

Famous Passages

Mountain of the Lord's house will be higher . . . peoples will
stream toward it—4:1–2
Swords into pruning hooks—4:3
Nation will not take up sword against nation; never be trained for
war—4:3
Each man will sit under his own vine—4:4
I shall assemble the dispersed . . . restore the lost remnant . . . turn
the outcasts into a mighty nation—4:7

Lord requires of you to act justly, to love loyalty, to walk humbly
with your God—6:8

NAHUM

PROPHECY

The prophet Nahum was also a poet who used metaphor
and imagery to convey his message. He wrote during a
time when world politics created major changes, which
he believed would have a positive impact on the people.
He declared that the people will witness Assyria, which
had ruled the region oppressively, and Nineveh, its capital
city, overpowered by Babylon. Nahum felt that Nineveh
was to receive the punishment it deserved and expected
peace to return to the land. He seemed unaware of the
threat that Babylon would present (they would overthrow
Jerusalem decades later), and fails to spell out the consequences of the divine justice for Israel itself, perhaps due
to his resoluteness of purpose.

Outline

The vengeance of God (1:1–11); Israel and Judah rid of the
Assyrian invaders (1:12–2:2); Nineveh is destroyed (2:1–3:19).

Famous Passages

The Lord is a jealous God, a God of vengeance—1:2
On the mountains are the feet of the herald who proclaims good
news!—1:15

✤ ✤ ✤ ✤

HABAKKUK

PROPHECY

We know nothing about Habakkuk other than the likely time of this book's writing—after Babylon overthrew Israel and continued to conquer neighboring countries. The book begins by questioning the justice of God: How can God allow a wicked nation like Babylon to conquer Israel? It then affirms that God's justice will be evident in the future and identifies the need for human confidence in God. Babylon will face its own day of judgment, the prophet argues; the people of Israel must live by faith and continue to live righteously.

Outline

Questions of how God can allow the wicked to triumph (1–2:3); denouncing human injustice (2:4–20); Psalm/prayer (3).

Famous Passages

How long, Lord, will you be deaf to my plea?—1:2–4
The Lord God is my strength; he makes me as sure-footed as a hind, sets my feet on the heights—3:19

ZEPHANIAH

PROPHECY

During the time when Babylon overthrew Assyria, but before they invaded the southern kingdom, Josiah, the king, embarked on religious reformation in Judah (2 Kings 22:1–23:30). Zephaniah wrote that corrupt, oppressive rulers would be destroyed and the land given to poor. He also talked about the coming day of the Lord and held up a vision of future glory.

Outline

Doom on Judah (1:4–18) and neighbors (2:1–15) because their leaders did not maintain the practices of the faith (1:4–6; 3:4–5) and oppressed the common people (3:1–3). God will destroy them and give the land to the humble and poor (3:11–20).

Famous Passages

I shall deal with all who oppress you . . . shall gather you and bring you home—3:12–20

HAGGAI

PROPHECY

The two chapters of this brief book contain four oracles (communications from God) that urge people to rebuild the temple in Jerusalem after the Exile in Babylon which ended about 539 BCE. The material in the book was composed in 520 BCE. During the first twenty years the people focused on rebuilding homes and the economy, but did little about their religious faith. Their first efforts at rebuilding the temple under Amos and Nehemiah's leadership had been stopped by the Persian authorities. As the Lord directs him, Haggai plaintively asked, "Is it a time for you yourselves to live in your paneled houses, while this house [of the Lord] lies in ruins?" Believing piety and prosperity were closely linked, Haggai urged the people to rebuild the temple, promising economic renewal as well. The rebuilding of the temple started within a month of his first oracle and was finished four years later.

Outline

The first oracle: the prophet urges the people to resume the rebuilding of the temple (1); second oracle: he encourages the builders to continue in the face of discouragement (2:1–9); third oracle: rebuke and promise given on the day the foundation is laid (2:10–19); fourth oracle: a word to the governor Zerubbabel, whom Haggai considered to be chosen by God to be a future ruler in the line of David (2:20–23).

Famous Passages

Because my house lies in ruins while each of you has a house he can hurry to—1:9

Begin the work, for I am with you . . . and my spirit remains among
you. Do not be afraid.—2:4–5

ZECHARIAH

PROPHECY

This book comes from the hand of more than one prophet. Zechariah, whose prophecies date from 520 to 518 BCE and are found in Zechariah 1–8, was a contemporary of Haggai (see p. 78). The remaining chapters of the book (which nowhere claim to be from Zechariah) assume a different setting; instead of Joshua and Zerubbabel, unnamed shepherds lead the community. And instead of peace and rebuilding, there are expectations of warfare and the siege of Jerusalem, placing them later, perhaps in the fourth, fifth, and even second century BCE. But Zechariah's earlier messianic themes (i.e. prophecies having to do with a coming Messiah or deliverer) are continued in these later chapters. Christians find many prophetic foreshadowings of the coming Christ in a number of verses.

Outline

Zechariah's commission and eight visions (1–6); six oracles about the coming age (7–8); Judah's triumph over enemies (9–11); Jerusalem to a center of worship for all (12–14).

Famous Passages

Administer justice, show kindness and compassion . . . do not oppress the widow, fatherless, alien or poor—7:9

Your king is coming to you . . . mounted on a donkey, on a colt,
    the foal of a donkey—9:9
I took the thirty pieces of silver . . . threw them into the house of
    the Lord, into the treasury—11:12–13
They will look on him whom they have pierced—12:10

MALACHI

PROPHECY

Malachi means "my messenger." The term may not be a personal name at all, but a title. And indeed, the task of this prophetic book is to bring two messages: God is displeased with the people's lack of piety and proper temple worship, and God is about to send a messenger or prophet ("Elijah") to unite the people before "the great and terrible day of the Lord comes" (4:5).

While the Judeans have returned from exile and rebuilt the temple (see Haggai and Zechariah), they still lived under the rule of Persia. To their adherence to the Law of Moses, therefore, was added the burden of following other laws governing civil and religious life. The prophetic call to faithfulness amid this tension set the stage for the development of legalism in Judaism but also fostered strong religious devotion during this time.

Outline

Religious decline and hope of recovery (1–3:12); the righteous
    triumphant (3:13–4:5). First oracle (1:2–5); second oracle
    (1:6–2:9); third oracle (2:10–16); fourth oracle (2:17–3:5);
    fifth oracle (3:6–12); sixth oracle (3:13–4:3).

Famous Passages

I will send my messenger to clear a path before me . . . who can
  endure the day of his coming? . . . he is like a refiner's fire . . .
  testing and purifying—3:1–2
"Bring the full tithe into the storehouse"—4:10
I will send you the prophet Elijah before the great and terrible day
  of the Lord comes.—4:5

THE
APOCRYPHA

Or Deuterocanonical Scriptures

The Apocrypha is an eclectic collection of writings that falls roughly into the time period between the Hebrew Bible and the New Testament. While some books in the Apocrypha probably were written earlier than some of the books in the Hebrew Bible, the three main history books (1 Esdras, 1 and 2 Maccabees) provide a historical record of intertestamental times. Of these three, 1 Maccabees is the most straightforward historical account; 2 Maccabees dramatizes the accounts and 1 Esdras uses the historical story to instruct the reader or to demonstrate religious truths the writer wants the reader to understand.

These three books comprise the bulk of the apocryphal writings. The rest of the Apocrypha is made up of various types of literature and even segments of books. 2 Esdras is apocalyptic in nature while Ecclesiasticus (also known as the Wisdom of Jesus Son of Sirach) and the Wisdom of Solomon are part of Israel's tradition of wisdom literature. Five of the books contain fascinating and fanciful stories (Tobit, Judith, Additions to Esther, Susanna, and Bel and the Snake). The Prayer of Manasseh stands as one of the most powerful prayers of confession in the biblical record.

Most of these books bear little or no relation to one another, and some, such as the Additions to Esther, make sense only if they are read with their companion book in the Hebrew Bible. Others, especially 1 Esdras, give us valuable insights into the time between the rise of the Maccabean family to political power (c. 165 BCE)[13] and the time when the Romans were in power as was true when the New Testament was written.

The books of the Apocrypha will generally be set apart in Protestant Bibles while Roman Catholic editions will intersperse most of the books (except 1 and 2 Esdras, the Prayer of Manasseh, and Psalm 151) among the books of the Hebrew Bible. To make things more confusing, some editions of the Bible use different numbering systems or put sections of books into appendixes (for example, in the Latin Vulgate, Ezra and Nehemiah are called 1 and 2 Esdras, thus renumbering the two books in the Apocrypha 3 and 4 Esdras!). The Orthodox Church also includes 3 and 4 Maccabees and Psalm 151 (included in *The Harper-Collins Study Bible* but not in *The Oxford Study Bible*).

Descriptions, Outlines, and Famous Passages

Symbols indicate level of difficulty: from ✲ (relatively easy reading) to ✲ ✲ ✲ ✲ ✲ (difficult reading, for experienced readers).

---

[13]*The Interpreter's One Volume Commentary on the Bible,* page 1110.

586 – 500	500 – 332	332 – 250	250 – 150	150 – 63
Period of Exile	Jews Return from Exile	Rise of Hellenism	Jews Under Hellenism	Roman Empire Expands

1 ESDRAS

NARRATIVE

Esdras comes from the Greek form of the Hebrew name Ezra. With some minor discrepancies and rearrangement, and with the exception of the story of a debate at the Persian court, the material in this book can be found in 2 Chronicles, Ezra, and Nehemiah. The purpose of this particular compilation is unclear, but the compiler seems eager to emphasize the role of King Josiah, the princely leader Zerubbabel, and the priest Ezra in reforming Israelite worship.

Outline

Reign of Josiah, exile in Babylon and return (1–2); debate at the Persian court (3–5:6); return from Babylon (5); rebuilding the temple (6–7); Ezra's story (8–9).

Famous Passages

What is strongest: wine, the king, women, or truth? 3:1–4:41

2 ESDRAS

APOCALYPTIC LITERATURE

Like the Book of Daniel, 2 Esdras is largely apocalyptic, that is, filled with a style of writing that uses visions and symbolic language to convey current and future realities. The middle of the book (3–14) contains Ezra's seven visions, which are surrounded by later additions. Scholars believe that portions of the book (e.g. chapters 1–2 and 15–16) were of Christian authorship dating from the second century CE. The book focuses on the fall of Jerusalem and life under Roman rule but also addresses the general problem of why people suffer. It holds out restitution and rewards in the world to come.

Outline

Preface about Israel's rejection and future glory (1–2); first vision: why does God allow suffering imposed by wicked people? (3–5:19); second vision: questions about the end times (5:20–6:59); third vision: the angel's response (7–9:25); fourth vision: the woman in mourning (9:26–10:58); fifth vision: the eagle and lion (11–12); sixth vision: the Messiah (13); seventh vision: sacred books written (14); conclusion: prophecies and warnings (15–16).

Famous Passages

I shall withdraw my presence from Israel, and the home that was to be theirs forever I shall give to my people—2:11

Champion the widow, defend the fatherless, give to poor, provide clothing, care for the weak, watch over the disabled—2:20–22

Survey of Israelite history—3:4–29

Creation story—6:35–59

Woman mourns death of son—9:38–10:28

TOBIT

WISDOM LITERATURE

This remarkable piece of historical fiction about a blind man, Tobit, was designed to encourage faithful Jews to follow his example. Despite many misfortunes and trials, Tobit remained faithful to God and the Torah. In the end he was healed and joined in celebrating his son's wedding, giving thanks that his line would be continued.

Outline

Tobit is taken into captivity (1); Tobit is blinded (2); each of Sarah's seven husbands die on their wedding days (3); Tobit's son, Tobias, is sent to retrieve Tobit's money from a friend (4); the angel Raphael guides Tobias (5–6); Tobias meets and weds Sarah (7–9); Tobias and Sarah return home (10); Tobit is healed (11), celebrates (12), offers a prayer of thanksgiving (13), and dies (14).

Famous Passages

Tobias and Sarah's Wedding Prayer—8:4–9

JUDITH

STORY

In the setting of this story, Assyria was conquering nations and Judah was being invaded. The city of Bethulia was about to fall, when Judith and her maid implemented a scheme to beguile the enemy commander Holofernes, get him drunk, and then kill him. The success of this plan resulted in the flight of the enemy and the salvation of Jerusalem. The story demonstrates God's commitment to the survival of the Jewish people and the importance of the people's faithfulness.

Outline

Assyrian conquests (1–3); the Israelites resist but are failing (4–6); Bethulia is about to surrender (7) when the widow Judith calls the leaders to faith in God (8), prays (9), and goes to the enemy commander (10–11). She seduces him to entertain her in his tent (12) and while he is drunk beheads him (13). She returns his head to the city and directs the men in battle (14–15). Judith offers a hymn of thanksgiving at a feast in Jerusalem (16).

Famous Passages

The Lord Almighty has thwarted them by a woman's hand—16:6

ESTHER

NARRATIVE

These chapters were written in Greek and added to the end of the original Hebrew book of Esther. The story is essentially the same as the Hebrew version, but does add more religious elements (the canonical book of Esther never mentions God). The arrangement of material may vary with different translations; the outline below gives the Greek sequence but with the chapter and verse numbers of the King James Version (see *The Oxford Study Bible* for a detailed explanation).

Outline

Mordecai has a dream (11) and discovers a plot against the king (12:1–6); Esther becomes Persian queen after Queen Vashti is dethroned (1–2); Mordecai is rewarded for saving the king's life (2:19–23) and refuses to bow to Haman (3:1–6). Haman gets royal edict to kill all Jews (3:7–13:7); Esther is asked to intervene (4); Mordecai's prayer (13); Esther's prayer (14); Esther goes to king (15) and gives a banquet while Haman prepares gallows to kill Mordecai (5); Haman is required to honor Mordecai (6); Esther requests that Jews be spared; king kills Haman in anger (7) and nullifies edict (8) as written in a letter (16); Jews take vengeance on their enemies (9:1–18) and establish the feast of Purim (9:20–32).

Famous Passages

Establishment of the feast of Purim and sending presents to friends and the poor—9:20–32

THE WISDOM OF SOLOMON

WISDOM LITERATURE

The author speaks in the name of King Solomon but was probably an Alexandrian Jew who wrote in Greek in a time when many Jews questioned or abandoned their faith. It identifies Wisdom with the Spirit of the Lord, describes a religious philosophy of history, and affirms reward and punishment after death.

Outline

God rewards the righteous and punishes the ungodly (1–5); the nature of wisdom (6–9); wisdom in Israel's history (10–11); God's mercy (12); the folly and results of idolatry (13–14); the benefits of worshiping God (15); a theology of history (16–19).

Famous Passages

Wisdom shuns ''a shifty soul,'' falsehood, unreason, injustice—1:4–5

Do not court death by a crooked life . . . God did not make death, takes no pleasure in the destruction of any living thing—1:12–16

The souls of the just are in God's hand—3:1

The true beginning of wisdom is the desire to learn—6:17

⚜ ⚜ ⚜ ⚜ ⚜

ECCLESIASTICUS

Also known as the Wisdom of Jesus Son of Sirach

WISDOM LITERATURE

"**A**ll wisdom is from the Lord," chapter 1 begins. Similar to Proverbs, Sirach, as this work is sometimes called, seeks to discover patterns and meaning in human life and concludes that wisdom is a gift of God. It contains commonsense advice about how to live with God and one another. The Hebrew language edition of this book was used as a school textbook, so segments of it were copied in many languages with teachers inserting explanatory notes, revisions, and even additions. The NRSV gives you some of these variations in the footnotes and italicized text in chapters 29 and 51. The Greek translation has been preserved in a more complete form.

The book is signed by its author, Jesus son of Sirach. Ben Sira (Sirach) was a scholar and teacher in Jerusalem sometime between 200 and 180 BCE. He combines typical Israelite and Near Eastern wisdom traditions with the commandments in the Torah to "support the Second Temple system of governance with its priestly codes of law and sacrifice."[14]

Outline

Prologue (unnumbered); source, definition, and signs of wisdom
(1); role of testing and experience (2); respect for parents
(3:1–16); need for humility (3:17–24); leadership and
responsibility to poor (4); reliance on God (5); wisdom in
relationships (5:9–10:3); exercise of wisdom (10:4–16:23);
God as Creator (16:17–18:14); self-control (18:15–19:17);
silence and speech (20); the importance of repentance (21);

[14]*The HarperCollins Study Bible, NRSV,* page 1531.

wise commentary on daily living (22); prayer for self-control (22:27–23:6); warnings against adultery (23:16–27); in praise of wisdom (24:1–25:11); home life and family relations (25:13–34:12); true piety (34:13–36:17); life in society (36:18–42:14); wonders of creation (42:15–43:33); Israel's heroes (44–50); epilogue (51).

Famous Passages

The beginning of wisdom is the fear (reverent acceptance) of the Lord—1:14

You that fear the Lord, wait for his mercy . . . trust in him . . . hope for prosperity, lasting joy—2:7–9

Look after your father in his old age; do nothing to grieve him—3:12–14

Do not cheat a poor person of his livelihood . . . drive him to desperation . . . turn your back on him—4:1–10

BARUCH

PRAYERS AND HYMNS

The book was named for Baruch, the prophet Jeremiah's secretary, but likely written at a later time. This anthology of prayers and hymns gives us an understanding of Jewish worship practices within one to two hundred years before the birth of Jesus.

Outline

Introduction (1:1–14); confession (1:15–22); lament (2:1–3:8); a hymn in praise of wisdom (3:9–4:4); poems and/or songs (4:5–5:9).

Famous Passages

Incline your ear to us, Lord, and hear; for the dead cannot sing the
Lord's praise—2:16–18

THE LETTER OF JEREMIAH

EPISTLE

This letter is a one-chapter diatribe against idolatry that
might have been a sermon written between one and
three hundred years before Jesus. The original language
and origins are unclear, though the writing's Semitic sentence construction suggests Hebrew or Aramaic origins.
Some English translations include it as the final (sixth)
chapter of Baruch (see p. 91).

Outline

The folly of idolatry (6:1–73).

Famous Passages

Other gods cannot set up kings, bestow wealth, save one from
death, rescue the weak, restore sight, redress
injustice—6:34–38; 53–57

THE PRAYER OF AZARIAH AND THE SONG OF THE THREE

POETRY

These two parts, probably independent, are additions to the Book of Daniel. Azariah is Abednego's Hebrew name; he was one of the three friends of Daniel that were thrown into the fire and survived.

Outline

Azariah's prayer (1:1–27); a song of exaltation (1:28–68).

Famous Passages

For the sake of your honor do not abandon us—1:11
Bless the Lord, sun and moon—1:40

SUSANNA

STORY

A story about Daniel and Susanna written as an addition to the Book of Daniel. Susanna, a beautiful married woman, was desired by two elders who spied on her as she bathed. When they attempted to rape her, she cried out for help. When her neighbors arrived, the elders said they discovered a young man with her. She was tried for adultery. At the witness of the two elders, she was convicted and sentenced to die. An indignant Daniel demanded a retrial and separated the men, whose stories did not match. They were then convicted of giving false evidence and put to death.

Outline

See paragraph above.

DANIEL, BEL, AND THE SNAKE

STORIES

These two tales as additions to the Book of Daniel are designed to ridicule idolatry. In the first story Daniel refuses to bow to the Babylonian idol Bel. The king ordered his priests to prove that it was a god. They set out food and planned to remove it through a hidden door. But Daniel sifted ashes over everything so the priests' footprints would be visible, exposing not only their deception but the folly of idol worship. In the second story it was a serpent that was worshiped. Daniel cleverly fed it a cake of pitch, fat, and hair which caused it to explode. Daniel was thrown into the lions' pit but was not eaten during the seven days. His detractors were then thrown in and promptly consumed.

Outline

The Bel story (1:1–22); the serpent (dragon) story (1:23–42).

THE PRAYER OF MANASSEH

PRAYER

King Manasseh engaged in idolatry, human sacrifice, and violence (see 2 Kings 21:1–18). After being held captive in Babylon he repented of his evil, was restored as king, and instituted reforms (see also 2 Chronicles 33:1–20). This brief prayer (15 verses) expresses sincere repentance and deep religious feeling.

Outline

God is praised (1–8); the king offers repentance (9–13a) and declares his confidence in divine mercy (13b–15).

Famous Passages

"I have sinned, Lord, I have sinned" (12–15)

PSALM 151

POEM/HYMN

This Psalm has not been a part of the currently known Jewish canon. However, the Greek and Syriac translations were accepted by the Eastern Orthodox Church and in 1956 it was found on a Hebrew scroll of biblical Psalms in Qumran Cave 11.[15] For these reasons it is included in the NRSV of the Bible (Note: *The HarperCollins Study Bible* includes this Psalm while other editions do not.)

Outline

Poetic comment on the anointing of David in 1 Samuel 16:1–13
    (1–4) and on David's slaying of the Philistine giant, Goliath
    (5–8)

Famous Passages

It is he who . . . anointed me—4

1, 2, 3, AND 4 MACCABEES

NARRATIVE

The first book is an account of the revolt against the kings of Syria which began in 167 BCE. Maccabee referred to the Jewish guerrillas who fought under the leadership of the priest Mattathias and later his son, Judas Maccabeus. The second book is a shortened version of a five-volume history by Jason of Cyrene (now lost) plus two letters. It shares elements with "pathetic history," a style of writing meant to arouse sympathy that used invented material, miracles, and exaggeration.

3 and 4 Maccabees have nothing to do with the Maccabees and were probably given this name only because they

[15]*The HarperCollins Study Bible, NRSV,* page 1749.

followed 1 and 2 Maccabees. 3 and 4 Maccabees are not accepted by the Roman Catholic or Protestant churches but is accepted by the Eastern Orthodox churches. (Note: They are included in *The HarperCollins Study Bible, NRSV,* but not in many other editions.) 3 Maccabees describes the life of being a religious minority trying to observe Jewish law and the loyal subjects of the king. 4 Maccabees is a philosophical discussion of the importance of "religious reason" over emotions designed to persuade the readers to observe the law even in extremely difficult circumstances.

Outline

1 MACCABEES

Background to the revolt (1); Mattathias begins armed resistance, dies (2); his son, Judas Maccabeus, leads Jews in war (3–9:22); Jonathan becomes leader and high priest (9:23–12); Simon becomes a leader (13–15) and is succeeded by his son John (16).

2 MACCABEES

Preface (1–2:18); summary of the five books (2:19–32); Syrian oppression of the Jews (3–7); Judas Maccabeus revolts (8–9); temple rededicated (10–15:16); the Jews triumph (15:17–39).

3 MACCABEES

Egyptian king wins battle, attempts to enter temple (1:1–15); Jews reaction (1:16–2:20); king is punished and lays demands on Jews (2:21–3:30); Jews imprisoned (4); king plots to annihilate the Jews (5); Eleazar prays, king repents (6); king's letter and departure (7).

4 MACCABEES

Author's topic of demonstrating supremacy of reason (1); law and reason are compatible (2); example of King David's thirst and attempt on temple treasury (3:6–4:26); the martyrdoms of

Eleazar (5:1–7:23); the seven brothers (8:1–14:10) and their mother (14:1–18:19).

Famous Passages

Mattathias's speech and murder of Jew making a pagan sacrifice—1 Maccabees 2:19–28

Jews flee to the desert and are killed—2:29–38

Five books summarized in one—2 Maccabees—2:23–24

Prayer of the High Priest Simon—3 Maccabees 2:1–20

Supremacy of reason—4 Maccabees 1:13–35

THE NEW TESTAMENT

(Also known as the Christian Testament)

The New Testament records the story of the life, teachings, death, and resurrection of Jesus Christ as well as the rise of the early Christian community. The word *testament* means "covenant," and the idea of a new covenant relationship between God and the people is seen in Jeremiah: "I will make a new covenant with the house of Israel and the house of Judah" (31:31). Christians see this new covenant as being inaugurated and made effective in and through Jesus Christ (see Hebrews 8 and 9).

Gospels

The New Testament contains two primary types of literature—Gospels and Epistles. The word *gospel* means "good news" or "glad tidings" and referred to Jesus as the ultimate redemption the prophets promised would come. It conveys the message of salvation (rescue and deliverance) proclaimed by Christians.

Between 70 and 100 CE, several authors compiled stories, sayings, and traditions by and about Jesus into narratives that came to be known as Gospels (probably because Mark's begins with the words *the beginning of the good news about Jesus Christ*).

Four Gospels made it into the New Testament canon.

Each was written from a particular perspective and with a different purpose. It is possible to discern an older source document or documents that Matthew, Mark, and Luke all used by looking at a Gospel parallel (a book with the same passage in three columns) and identifying where the same words are used in the different Gospels. Mark is the shortest, oldest, and simplest Gospel to read. Some of the additional material in Matthew and Luke seems to come from an older common document (sometimes labeled "Q") or from separate records of various stories and sayings.

Because these stories and sayings originally were told orally, we cannot be certain when they began to be recorded or by whom. It appears that compiling a complete record became important to the early Christians as the last eyewitnesses to the events related to Jesus died and the next generation assumed responsibility for transmitting the story. While there is some variation in emphasis, perspective, and arrangement of material, the Synoptic Gospels (Matthew, Mark, and Luke) are remarkably similar. John uses a very different writing style to convey the same message. In all four Gospels the purpose is the same: "these are written so that you may come to believe that Jesus is the Messiah, the Son of God, and that through believing you may have life in his name" (John 20:31).

The Jesus Story

The Gospels establish Jesus' lineage to King David, a requisite for him to be "the Messiah," the one who would deliver Israel. They describe how he was baptized in a river by John the Baptist at about thirty years of age and there confirmed by God as "my beloved son."

After forty days of wilderness fasting (a prelude and preparation for his public ministry), Jesus was tempted by Satan. After emerging victorious, Jesus launched a ministry of teaching, healing, and miracle working, all interpreted in unique ways by each of the four Gospels. We also read of a recurring element of Jesus' teaching—his parables (enigmatic stories with a powerful punch line). Many people saw him as a rabbi (Jewish teacher) or a prophet, but some believed he was none other than Israel's awaited messianic deliverer.

While Jesus was popular with the people, his teachings (and popularity) challenged civic and (especially) religious leaders. What he did and said was so radical that the authorities ultimately had him killed to silence him. While the Gospel writers did not explain all the tensions Jesus created (likely assuming that they were obvious to their contemporaries), they did spend considerable time recording the remarkable experiences after Jesus' death. His crucifixion,[16] resurrection from the dead, and subsequent supernatural appearances transformed his disciples[17] from a scattered group of followers into a people who proclaimed God's new relationship with humanity with power and conviction. The disciples became "a people"—the Christian community.

Epistles

A significant portion of the New Testament consists of Epistles—letters—usually written to a Christian group that met in a specific community. They sometimes served to introduce the bearer to a new community. In many cases they were written by Paul, the church's primary missionary to the Gentiles,[18] to the churches he had started in different cities.

For Paul and the early Christian leaders, epistles became a primary means of expressing early Christian theology (systematic thoughts about God). They repeat some of the story of Jesus found in the Gospels, but mostly they

[16]An especially painful and protracted method of execution by nailing victims to a cross, where they usually died of suffocation.

[17]The word literally means "learner" but gained a special meaning that referred to those who apprenticed themselves to teachers.

[18]Non-Jews.

reflect on what that story meant, what it said about God's relationship with humanity, and what it said about how we should live in relationship with God and one another.

Canonizing the Story

It is important to remember that Jesus, his followers, and many members of the early church were Jews. The Hebrew Bible was their only Bible. The story of Jesus initially was told to others, not written. And most of the early written materials were personal letters.

Gradually the church began to identify the Gospels and epistles and other writings as another body of Scriptures, which became the New Testament. The first time we see a list that matches the current list of twenty-seven books is in 367 CE in Athanasius's Festal Letter.

As happened in Hebrew Scriptures, a key event laid behind the formation of the New Testament—in this case the death and resurrection of Jesus Christ:[19]

1. This "core narrative" was told at every celebration of the Eucharist and during Holy Week/Easter, the primary Christian festival.
2. The Gospels (Matthew, Mark, Luke, and John) and some of Paul's Epistles expand the core narrative and continue to record the story (between about 70 and 140 CE).
3. The later Epistles (e.g. 1, 2, and 3 John, 1 and 2 Timothy, Titus, 2 Peter) demonstrate how this narrative grew more formalized in creeds. They also show the Christian community becoming more organized.
4. Liturgy and songs (e.g. Songs of Mary, Zechariah, and Simeon in Luke; Songs to the Lamb and of the Redeemed in Revelation) become part of the sacred story.
5. A vision of the future takes firm shape (Hebrews and Revelation of John).

[19]The following understanding of how sacred story was formed is based on work by Joseph Russell.

While the Hebrew Scriptures cover thousands of years of history and were written over hundreds of years, the New Testament covers only about a hundred years and was written within a span of about 150 years. In both cases there were many books to choose from and the process of selecting which books would be officially recognized as Scripture took several hundred years. During that time, various editions of each book were circulated and translations were made into different languages, a situation not unlike our contemporary multiplication of versions and translations.

The Christian Story

The books of the Hebrew Bible tell the story of the Hebrew people, their relationship with God, and the development of the Jewish faith. The books of the New Testament tell the story of Jesus Christ, the relationship he and his followers had with God, and the development of the Christian faith.

The New Testament builds on Hebrew Scripture just as Christianity builds on Judaism. For Christians, Jesus is God incarnate: "God made man." Jesus is the Torah made flesh and blood; he is the new temple, the Divine Wisdom, the Lamb of God in the Passover feast, the Suffering Servant in Isaiah, the Messiah—all titles and concepts from the Hebrew Bible.

Christ created a new relationship between God and humanity which can be summed up by John 3:16–17: "God so loved the world that he gave his only Son, so that everyone who believes in him may not perish but may have eternal life. Indeed, God did not send the Son into the world to condemn the world, but in order that the world might be saved through him."

In Christ, God became "incarnate"—the divine became human. The relationship between God and humanity is also "incarnate." Christ "dwells" or "abides" in us and we dwell in Christ (John 15:4, 1 John 3:24) and God dwells in us and we in God (1 John 4:15–16).

Christianity focuses on love as the primary commandment or rule of life—love God "with all your heart . . . soul . . . mind . . . strength . . . [and] love your neighbor as yourself" (Mark 12:29–31). Through the Holy Spirit, given by Christ, Christians are united with God and one another. That Spirit works in and through people, enabling them to speak God's word with power and be instruments for healing and wholeness. As such they participate in Christ's work of reconciliation, of bringing people into unity with God and one another in Christ. This unity, this eternal oneness with God, who is love, is "salvation."

Descriptions, Outlines, and Famous Passages

Symbols indicate level of difficulty: from ✴ (relatively easy reading) to ✴ ✴ ✴ ✴ ✴ (difficult reading, for experienced readers only).

38 – 4 BCE	4 BCE – 30 CE	30 CE – 69	70 – 100	100 – 135
Palestine Ruled By Herod	Life of Jesus	Early Church & Paul	Fall of Jerusalem; Spread of Christianity	New Testament Completed

[✤]

MATTHEW

GOSPEL

Written about 90 CE, this Gospel tells the story of Jesus from a Jewish perspective and is probably addressed to Jewish converts. Jesus picked twelve of his many disciples (learners who followed Jesus) to be his "apostles"—those sent to be teachers. Matthew, sometimes called Levi, is one of them. He was a tax collector, despised because he was seen as helping the Romans oppress the Jews.

Matthew starts with a genealogy and quotes the Hebrew prophecies of old to show the relationship between Jesus and God's ancient promises to the Jewish people. He addressed the growing sense that Christ's return in glory was not likely to happen as quickly as first thought. His Gospel is a manual of Christian teachings, administration, discipline, and worship that responds to the question of how Christians should live in the meantime.

Matthew is unique in organizing Jesus' teachings into five discourses, including the Sermon on the Mount (chapters 5–7), the longest single piece of Jesus' teaching in the Bible. The Gospel seems to be patterned after the Torah with the five discourses matching the five Deuteronomic books. The trip of Jesus' parents to Egypt, for instance, echoes the Hebrew Egyptian captivity, and Jesus' teaching on the mountain parallels the giving of the Mosaic Law on Mount Sinai.

Outline

Genealogy of the Messiah (1:1–17); birth of Jesus, flight into Egypt (1:18–2:23); Jesus' baptism (3); his temptations (4:1–11); his beginning of public ministry and calling of his disciples (4:12–28); teachings in five great discourses: first, the Sermon on the Mount (5–7); second (missionary), the commissioning of the Twelve (10); third, parables on "the kingdom is like" (13); fourth, church discipline (18); and fifth (eschatological), destruction of the temple, signs, warnings, and parables about the end times (24–25); crucifixion (26–27); resurrection appearances and disciples' "great commission" (28).

Famous Passages

Birth of Jesus—1:18–2:23

John baptizes Jesus, "this is my beloved Son."—3:1–17

Temptation of Jesus in the wilderness—4:1–11

Call to Peter, Andrew, James, and John; "I will make you fishers of men."—4:12–25

Sermon on the Mount—5:1–7:29

Beatitudes—5:3–11

Lord's Prayer—6:9–13

Golden Rule—7:12

Jesus heals a person with leprosy, 8:1–4; the centurion's servant, 8:5–13; a paralytic, 9:2–8; a woman who is hemorrhaging, 9:20–22; the blind and mute, 9:27–33, 12:22–24; the Canaanite woman's daughter, 15:21–28

Foxes have holes . . . Son of Man has nowhere to lay his head—8:20

Jesus calms the storm at sea—8:23–26

Jesus casts out demons—8:28–34

Jesus chooses and commissions twelve apostles—10:1–42

Jesus and John the Baptist—11

Opposition to eating and healing on the Sabbath—12:1–14

Parables—chapters 13, 21, 22:1–14, 24:42–26:1

Jesus feeds thousands—14:13–21 and 15:32–39

Jesus walks on water—14:22–34

Peter names Jesus as Son of God; "on this rock I will build my church."—16:13–20

The transfiguration—17:1–8

Teachings about the kingdom—18

Marriage and divorce—19:3–12

Let the little children come to me—19:13–15

Sell your possessions, give to the poor, follow me—19:16–22
Laborers in the vineyard; last will be first—20:1–16
Jesus enters Jerusalem on donkey—21:1–10
Jesus throws money changers out of the temple—21:12–13
Great Commandment: love God and neighbor—22:34–39
Woman anoints Jesus with perfume—26:6–13
Passover/Last Supper—26:17–29
Jesus prays in Garden of Gethsemane; let this cup pass from me
    . . . your will be done—26:36–46
Jesus arrested—26:47–56
Jesus before Jewish authorities—26:57–75
Jesus before Roman governor, Pilate—27:1–26
Jesus is crucified, dies, and is buried—27:27–66
Women discover the risen Christ—28:1–20
Great commission to go to all nations, make them disciples,
    baptizing and teaching them—28:19–20

MARK

GOSPEL

The shortest and oldest of the Gospels, Mark was probably written during or shortly after the destruction of
the temple in 70 CE.[20] Mark's story of Jesus emphasizes
victory over demonic forces as seen especially in the stories of Jesus healing and casting out demons. It stresses
Jesus' suffering and death with clear implications that
Jesus' followers will also embrace self-sacrificial service.
Mark also includes scenes demonstrating the disciples'
lack of understanding of who Jesus was (his true identity),

---

[20]There are three temples built on the same site: the one Solomon
built, destroyed in 586 BCE; the one Zerubbabel built after the Exile
completed about 515 BCE (see Ezra and Nehemiah), and rebuilt version
started by Herod around 20 BCE and destroyed in 70 CE. The Muslim
Dome of the Rock now sits on this site. The Western Wall is still accessible in Jerusalem and is a sacred site for Jews.

as well as times when Jesus showed reluctance for word about his identity to spread prematurely.

Mark was written for Gentile readers at a time when the early Christians were beginning to face persecution under the Emperor Nero. Part of Mark's purpose seems to be to encourage his readers to remain faithful in the face of trouble. Mark also emphasizes that in Christ the reign of God has begun with new power. This Gospel is often read as an introductory overview of the story of Jesus.

Outline

Proclamation of the kingdom (1–3); parables of the kingdom of God (4:1–34); miracles (4:35–8:26); on discipleship (8:27–10:52); ministry in Jerusalem (11–12); warnings (13); crucifixion (14–15); the empty tomb and the risen Jesus (16).

Famous Passages

John the Baptist—1:1–8

Baptism of Jesus, "You are my Son"—1:9–11

Temptation of Jesus—1:12–13

Call to Peter, Andrew, James, John—1:16–20

Jesus casts out demons—1:21–28; 5:1–20; 7:24–30; 9:14–29

Jesus heals a man with leprosy, 1:40–45; a paralytic, 2:1–12; a man with withered hand, 3:1–6; a woman who is hemorrhaging, 5:25–34; a deaf man, 7:31–37; a blind man, 8:22–26; blind Bartimaeus, 10:46–52

Call of Levi (Matthew)—2:12–17

Jesus chooses twelve apostles—3:13–19

Parable of the sower—4:1–9

Lamp under a bushel basket—4:21–25

Parable of the mustard seed—4:30–32

Jesus still a storm—4:35–40

Jesus restores a girl to life—5:21–24, 35–43

Jesus feeds thousands—6:30–42; 8:1–10

Jesus walks on water—6:45–61

Peter recognizes Jesus as Messiah—8:27–30

LUKE

GOSPEL

The longest Gospel, Luke is the first part of a work that is continued in the Acts of the Apostles. It was written about 90 CE, most likely by and for Gentile Christians. Luke, whom tradition identifies as a physician, worked with Paul. He gathered accounts from people who knew Jesus and carefully arranged them so they would tell the story in a logical progression. Luke presents Jesus both as the culmination of God's promises to the Hebrew people and as a universal savior. Through the stories of Jesus he selects, Luke demonstrates special concern for prayer, the Holy Spirit, the outcast, and the role of women in the church.

Outline

Birth of John and Jesus, Jesus' childhood (1–2); John baptizes Jesus (3); Jesus in Galilee (4–6); miracles and parables (7–8); Jesus and the Twelve (9); to Jerusalem (9:51–11:13); opposition (11:14–14:35); parables of the lost sheep, lost coin, prodigal son (15); instruction (16–18); Jesus begins journey to Jerusalem (18:31–19:48); warnings (21); Last Supper (22); crucifixion (22:47–23:56); resurrection (24).

Famous Passages

Births of John and Jesus foretold—1:5–25
Magnificat (Mary's Song)—1:46–55
Birth of John the Baptist—1:57–80
Birth of Jesus—2:1–20
Jesus presented in temple—2:21–40
Jesus amazes teachers at age 12—2:41–52
Jesus baptized; "You are my Son."—3:21–22
Jesus tempted by Satan in wilderness—4:1–13
Jesus casts out demons—4:31–37; 8:26–39; 9:37–43
Jesus calls Simon Peter, James, John—5:1–11
Jesus heals leper, 5:12–16; paralytic, 5:17–26; centurion's servant, 7:1–10; woman who is hemorrhaging, 8:43–48; crippled woman, 13:10–17; ten lepers, 17:11–19; blind beggar, 18:35–43
Jesus returns boy to life, 7:11–17; girl, 8:40–42, 49–56
Opposition to eating, healing on Sabbath—6:1–10
Jesus chooses twelve apostles—6:12–16
Sermon on the Plain—6:17–49 (Matthew chapters 5–7)
Woman anoints Jesus' feet with oil; wipes with her hair; sins forgiven—7:36–50
Parable of Sower—8:4–15
Lamp under a jar—8:16–18

Jesus calms a storm—8:22–25
Jesus feeds thousands—9:10–17
Peter names Jesus as Messiah—9:18–21
The Transfiguration—9:28–36
Seventy sent, return—10:1–24
Parable of Good Samaritan—10:25–37
Mary and Martha with Jesus—10:38–42
Lord's Prayer—11:1–4
Do not worry, consider lilies—12:22–34
Parables of the Lost Sheep, Coin—15:1–10
Parable of Prodigal Son—15:11–32
Widow and unjust judge—18:1–8
Let the little children come to me—18:15–17
Sell, give to the poor, follow me—18:18–30
Parable of Ten Pounds (Talents)—19:11–27
Jesus enters Jerusalem on colt—19:28–39
Jesus throws out money changers—19:45–48
Widow's offering of all she had—21:1–4
Passover/Lord's Supper—22:7–23
Jesus arrested—22:47–53
Peter denies knowing Jesus—22:54–62
Jesus mocked—22:63–71
Jesus before Pilate, Herod; sentenced—23:1–25
Jesus is crucified, dies, and is buried—23:26–56
Women discover Christ is risen—24:1–12
Road to Emmaus story; Christ known in the breaking of the
    bread—24:13–35
Jesus appears to disciples—24:36–49
Jesus ascends to heaven—24:50–53

JOHN

GOSPEL

The Gospel of John uses imagery and symbols to give a theological interpretation of what Jesus did. The author gives attention to the spiritual significance of events and arranges his material so that the action happens around Jewish holy days. There is a focus on "signs" (acts of power by Jesus that point to a truth otherwise undiscernible) and "glory" (the manifestation of God's presence). John's material is arranged into "The Book of Signs" (1:19–12:50) and "The Book of Glory" (13:1–20:31) with a prologue and epilogue.

John covers far fewer events than the other Gospels, but explores the ones he records in much greater depth. For example, he devotes five chapters (13–17) to record what Jesus did and said the night before he died. Since this Gospel was written later, John can leave the basic story to the other Gospels and focus on the meanings behind the story. His writing style is more poetry than prose, giving even more layers of meaning to what he writes.

A tradition dating to the second century CE identifies the author of this Gospel as John, the son of Zebedee, one of Jesus' disciples, though a number of modern scholars have called that connection into question.

Outline

Coming of Christ (1); signs (2–4:42); Jesus: giver of life, bread of life (4:43–6); great controversy (7–8); seeing and believing (9); victory over death (10–11); Passover (11:55–12); farewell discourses (13–17); crucifixion (18–19); resurrection (20–21).

Famous Passages

In the beginning was the Word . . . was God . . . became flesh—1:1–4

John describes Jesus' baptism—1:29–34

Jesus calls Andrew, Simon Peter, Philip—1:35–43

Jesus changes water into wine at a wedding in Cana—2:1–11

Jesus throws money changers out of temple—2:13–25

Nicodemus; ''you must be born again.''—3:1–20

God loved world, gave Son, all who believe in him will be
    saved—3:16

Jesus and Samaritan woman—4:1–39

Jesus heals official's son, 4:46–54; cripple on Sabbath, 5:1–18

Jesus feeds thousands—6:1–15

Jesus walks on water—6:16–21

Jesus, the bread of life—6:22–59

Woman caught in adultery—8:1–11

Jesus, the light of the world—8:12–20

Man born blind receives sight; believes Jesus is Son of
    Man—9:1–41

Jesus, the Good Shepherd—10:1–21

Jesus restores Lazarus to life—11:1–44

Mary anoints Jesus with perfume—12:1–8

Jesus enters Jerusalem on colt—12:12–19

Jesus washes disciples' feet; serve as I have served you—13:1–20

New Commandment: Love—13:31–35

Promise of the Holy Spirit—14:15–31

Jesus, the True Vine—15:1–17

Love; lay down life for friend—15:12–13

Jesus arrested—18:1–11

Jesus before High Priest—18:12–14, 19–24

Peter denies Jesus—18:15–18, 25–27

Jesus before Pilate—18:28–40

Jesus sentenced, mocked—19:1–16

Jesus is crucified, dies, and is buried—19:17–42

Jesus appears to Mary—20:1–18

Jesus appears to disciples, Thomas—20:19–28

''Cast net on other side''; the miraculous catch of fish—21:1–14

Jesus tells Peter, feed my sheep—21:15–19

⚜ ACTS

NARRATIVE

The Acts of the Apostles picks up the threads begun in the Gospel of Luke by chronicling the beginnings of the Christian church. It places strong emphasis on the power of the Holy Spirit and shows how God continues to fulfill the divine plan to save us. The preaching of the apostles, accompanied by miraculous signs and recorded at some length, showed how God's covenant with the Hebrew people continued to be fulfilled in the life of the church through the Holy Spirit. Acts traces the development of the church from its inception at Pentecost[21] and its expansion from a Jewish nucleus in Jerusalem to the Gentile world and ultimately throughout the entire Roman empire. It records the ministry of Peter and especially Paul, the early church's chief evangelist, and contains one of the key debates of the early church: should Gentiles be allowed into the church without becoming Jews first?

Outline

Jesus' ascension and the creation of the church in Jerusalem (1–5); Pentecost (2); selection of deacons (6); Stephen is stoned to death (7); Saul (Paul) persecutes Christians, is converted (8–9); Peter and the Gentiles (10–12); Paul's first missionary journey to Gentiles (13–14); the apostolic council in Jerusalem (15); Paul's second missionary journey (15:36–18:22) and third journey (18:23–21:17); his arrest in Jerusalem (21:27–22:29); his trials (22:30–26); and journey to Rome (27–28).

[21]The day of the outpouring of the Spirit on the people who praised God in many voices. Sometimes it is called the "Birthday of the Church."

Famous Passages

Jesus ascends to heaven—1:1–11
Pentecost, Peter's sermon, early converts—2:1–47
Peter heals crippled beggar—3:1–9
Believers share possessions—4:32–37
Ananias and Sapphira lie and die—5:1–10
The apostles heal many—5:12–16; 9:32–35
Stephen's speech—7:1–53
Philip baptizes the Ethiopian eunuch—8:25–40
Saul (renamed Paul) is converted—9:1–19
Dorcas is restored to life—9:36–43
Peter's vision of what is clean and unclean, his meeting with
    Cornelius—10:1–33
Gentiles are converted, receive the Spirit—10:34–48
Angel frees Peter from prison—12:6–19
Paul and Barnabas sent out—13:1–3
Council in Jerusalem; Gentiles accepted without
    circumcision—15:1–21
Paul casts demon out of woman, is jailed, and then freed by
    earthquake; jailer converts—16:16–40
Paul's autobiography—26:4–29

ROMANS

EPISTLE TO THE CHURCH AT ROME

Paul uses this letter to introduce himself to the church in Rome, where he plans to visit, and explains his experiences and theology. This is not only Paul's longest Epistle, it is the weightiest and most influential of all his correspondence. It was likely written between 54 and 58 CE. One of his key themes centers around the good news of Christ as God's power for salvation to all who believe. Here he lays out in greatest detail his conviction that righteousness depends on faith as opposed to rigid adherence to law. As is the case with most of his Epistles, he closes the letter with ethical teaching and some personal remarks.

Outline

The Gospel of Christ (1–2); the Jews and the Law (3–4); baptism and life in Christ (5–6); Paul's perspective on role of law (7), life in Spirit (8), the place of Jews and Gentiles in God's plan (9–11), and the Christian life (12–15).

Famous Passages

No one justified by keeping the law—3:20

Is God the God of Jews only?—3:29–31

Abraham's faith counted as righteousness—4:3

Believers as justified by Christ's death and so reconciled to God—5:9–11

Believers as baptized into union with Christ's death and resurrection—6:1–11

I want to do right, but do wrong—7:21–25

We are God's adopted children—8:12–25

If God is for us, who is against us?—8:31

Nothing can separate us from the love of God in Christ Jesus—8:35–39

Offer yourselves as living sacrifices; do not be conformed, but transformed—12:1–2

Spiritual gifts, practices—12:6–21

Love sums up the Law—13:8–10

✳ ✳ ✳

1 AND 2 CORINTHIANS

EPISTLE TO THE CHURCH AT CORINTH

orinth was situated near the center of a major Roman province in one of the most important cities of Greece. Paul's first letter to the church there deals with issues of Christian living and offers a glimpse of how the first-century church wrestled with issues of discipline and forgiveness. It was written to settle arguments in the church and to answer questions. It addresses immorality, lawsuits, marriage, divorce, worship, and spiritual gifts. 1 Corinthians 13, a lyrical, moving meditation on love, is heard often at contemporary weddings.

The second letter may really be the third letter; the intervening one (the so-called "severe letter" alluded to by Paul in 2 Corinthians 2:4) has been lost, or fragments of it may have been merged into the middle of this letter (parts of chapters 10–13). The severe letter apparently chastised the church after his visit failed to resolve a disciplinary problem. This letter rejoices that the Corinthians have had a change of heart and urges forgiveness for the person who caused the first crisis.

Outlines

1 CORINTHIANS

Church conflicts (1–4); sexual immorality (5); lawsuits (6); marriage and divorce (7); worship (8–11); spiritual gifts (12–14); the resurrection of the dead (15); closing (16).

2 CORINTHIANS

Paul's concern for the church at Corinth (1–2:13); a description of his ministry of suffering (2:14–6:13); church life and discipline (6:14–7:16); collection for the church in Jerusalem (8–9);

challenge to Paul's authority and his response (10–12); closing (13).

Famous Passages

1 CORINTHIANS

Your body is a temple of the Holy Spirit—6:12–20
The Lord's Supper—11:23–26
Varieties of spiritual gifts; same Spirit—12:4–11
One body, many members—12:12–31
Love is patient, kind, not envious . . .—13
As all die in Adam, so all will be made alive in Christ—15:12–22

2 CORINTHIANS

God reconciled us to himself through Christ; gave us ministry of reconciliation—5:18–20
Give generously—8:1–15; 9:1–15

⁜ GALATIANS

EPISTLE TO THE CHURCHES AT GALATIA

"**Y**ou are freed from the law in order to act out of love" is Paul's message to a group of churches in Galatia. This letter spells out Paul's understanding of Christian behavior and the relationship of Jewish tradition and Christian revelation. In it we catch a glimpse of the conflict between the Jews who saw Christianity as a part of Judaism and continuous with Jewish ritual and custom, and those, like Paul, who saw it as God's good news of freedom from legalism. The reader can also detect undercurrents of conflict with the Jerusalem church, which was dominated by more rigidly Jewish Christians. Unlike the "Judaizers," who believed that converts had to become

Jews first (and submit to circumcision and other legal and ritual requirements), Paul claimed that faith in Christ was what makes one Christian. The establishment of the principles proclaimed in this letter paved the way for Christianity to become a world religion instead of remaining a subdivision of Judaism.

Outline

One Gospel for both Jews and Gentiles (1–2); role of faith and law (3–4:20); freedom through Christ (4:21–5:12); guidance by the Spirit and ethical responsibilities of faith and love (5:13–6:18).

Famous Passages

Justified through faith in Christ—2:15–21
No Jew or Greek, slave or free, male or female; all are one in Christ—3:28–29
You are God's adopted children—4:1–7
Fruit of the Spirit is love, joy, peace . . .—5:22–23
Bear one another's burdens—6:2
You reap what you sow—6:7–10

EPHESIANS

EPISTLE

This letter draws on powerful poetic language, perhaps from early Christian liturgies and hymns, to paint a grand vision of God's purposes in the coming of Christ and the creation of his church. It was likely sent to various churches in Asia Minor as a summary of Paul's "gospel." It shows that Jew and Gentile have been united in the church, the "body of Christ." An ethical exhortation stresses love as an outcome of faith and underscores the importance of sexual purity and family harmony. It also identifies gifts of the Spirit—divinely assisted abilities—and speaks of donning God's "armor" for "spiritual warfare." This book may have been written by Paul (while he was imprisoned) or by a disciple of his. Some scholars place its date at 61–63 CE; those who feel it was written by a member of the Pauline "school" date it around 100 CE.

Outline

Christ in the church (1); God's grace to Gentiles (2); Paul's prayer (3); Christian conduct (4–5:20); relationships (5:21–6:1); our spiritual armor (6:10–24).

Famous Passages

You have been saved through faith; not your doing but it is a gift from God—2:9

There is one body, one Spirit . . . one Lord, one faith, one baptism, one God of all—4:4–6

Spiritual gifts given to equip saints for the work of ministry; build up body of Christ—4:11–16

Be angry but do not sin; do not let the sun go down on your anger—4:26

Be imitators of God; live in love—5:1–2

Put on the whole armor of God—6:11–17

✛ ✛

PHILIPPIANS

EPISTLE TO THE CHURCH AT PHILIPPI

This was one of the first churches Paul founded. He writes from prison to encourage unity, warn against false teachings, and urge Christians to keep the faith in the face of opposition. It contains some of Paul's strongest and most poetic proclamations (e.g. 2:5–11) combined with obvious expressions of affection for a church with whom he had a warm and happy relationship. This may have originally been a single letter or three separate letters—a letter of concern about potentially disruptive persons (1:1–3a; 4:2–9, 21–23), a letter against false teachers (3:1b–4:1), and a note of thanks (4:10–23).

Outline

Paul in prison (1:1–26); call to unity (1:27–2:18); Paul's plans (2:19–3:1a); against false teachers (3); note of thanks and closing (4).

Famous Passages

Hymn of Christ who emptied himself, took form of slave, was obedient to death—2:5–11

Rejoice in the Lord always; do not worry; pray; the peace of God will guard you—4:4–7

✶✶✶

COLOSSIANS

EPISTLE TO THE CHURCH AT COLOSSAE

This book asserts the primacy of Christ over all; it was written because the Colossians were combining the Christian gospel with pagan and marginal Jewish elements. It may have been written by Paul or a disciple of his, probably 61–63 CE.

Outline

Opening (1:1–8); supremacy of Christ (1:9–2:5); warnings against false teaching (2:6–23); Christian behaviors (3:1–4:6); closing (4:7–18).

Famous Passages

Christ is the image of God; in him all things were
created . . .—1:15–20
Set your minds on things above—3:1–4
As God's chosen ones, holy and beloved clothe yourself with
love. . . .—3:12–17

✶✶✶✶

1 AND 2 THESSALONIANS

EPISTLE TO THE CHURCH AT THESSALONICA

Written to a church largely made up of converts from paganism, these letters describe the future coming of Christ (*parousia*) seen as imminent in 1 Thessalonians and more distant in 2 Thessalonians. The first letter was written to help Christians perplexed by the death of believers; some of the Thessalonians worried that those who died might be excluded from the resurrection of the dead. Paul reassures and urges them to live in constant readiness for that day. The second letter seems designed to head off excesses of waiting for the second coming. It stresses the importance of continuing the pursuits of daily life, especially work, in a regular and orderly way. It is likely that Paul wrote the first letter around 51 CE; the date (and indeed his authorship) of the second letter is not clear.

Outlines

1 THESSALONIANS

The church at Thessalonica (1–3); the need for moral purity and love (4:1–12); Christ's return (4:13–5:11); Paul's closing appeal (5:12–28).

2 THESSALONIANS

Introduction (1); calm readiness in awaiting Christ's return (2); injunctions against idleness and other admonitions to Christian behavior (3).

Famous Passages

1 THESSALONIANS

God has destined us not for wrath but for salvation through Christ—5:9–10
Do not repay evil for evil; do good—5:15
Pray without ceasing—5:17
Give thanks in all circumstances—5:18

2 THESSALONIANS

The Lord is faithful; he will strengthen you and guard you from the evil one—3:3
Anyone unwilling to work should not eat—3:10b

❋❋❋

1 AND 2 TIMOTHY

EPISTLE TO TIMOTHY

Paul's letters to Timothy provide instructions to the leaders of churches on how to exercise pastoral leadership. For this reason, these letters, together with Titus, are called the Pastoral Epistles. In the first letter to Timothy we see the development of formal leaders in the church, the bishop, and elders.

Because their language and style is quite different from the other letters, many scholars feel they were ascribed to Paul by a group who wrote about problems after Paul's death, responding to them in the way they thought he would have. They urge believers to live faithfully and devoutly, exercising proper Christian behaviors.

Outlines

1 TIMOTHY

Charge to Timothy (1); exhortations to pray (2); leadership in the church (3); counters to false teachings (4); church discipline (5); instructions (6).

2 TIMOTHY

The Gospel of Christ (1); how Timothy is to serve (2); standing firm in the face of troubles (3–4:8); personal closing (4:9–22).

Famous Passages

1 TIMOTHY

Christ came to save sinners—1:15
There is the one mediator between God and humankind, Christ Jesus—2:5–6

Everything created by God is good—4:4–5
The love of money is root of evil—6:10

2 TIMOTHY

If we died with him, we will also live with him—2:11–13
All scripture is inspired by God and is useful for
    teaching . . .—3:16–17
I have run the great race, finished the course, kept the
    faith—4:6–8

TITUS

EPISTLE TO TITUS

Instructions on Christian discipline and leadership addressed to Titus, a friend and colleague of Paul's who
worked in Crete. Titus went to the Apostolic Council
in Jerusalem with Paul (Galatians 2:1–10), helped collect
money for the poor in Jerusalem (2 Corinthians 8:6, 16–
24), and went to the church at Corinth to soothe their
reaction to a tough letter from Paul (2 Corinthians 7:5–
16). Although Crete is not mentioned elsewhere as one of
Paul's missionary sites, this letter assumes that Titus was
to organize churches Paul had recently established there.
Titus is the third letter of the Pastoral Epistles (see also
1 and 2 Timothy).

Outline

Opening (1:1–4); Christian discipline (1:5–3:8), closing (3:8–15).

Famous Passages

Speak evil of no one, avoid quarreling, be gentle, show
    courtesy—3:2

After two admonitions, have nothing to do with anyone who
   causes divisions—3:10

PHILEMON

EPISTLE TO PHILEMON

A very short personal letter written by Paul to persuade
Philemon to receive his runaway slave, Onesimus,
back as a Christian brother. The church in Colossians met
at Philemon's home, indicating that he was a leader in
that congregation. The normal penalty for a slave running
away was severe. Paul wrote to show how Christ affects
relationships—since Onesimus has become a Christian,
the two men are now brothers in Christ. While Paul does
not address the institution of slavery, he expects Philemon
to accept Onesimus without penalty and volunteers to pay
for anything he might owe. There is an implication that
Paul hopes Philemon will send Onesimus back to assist
Paul.

Outline

Opening (1–7); a plea for Onesimus (8–22); closing (23–25).

Famous Passages

No longer as a slave but more than a slave, a brother—16

HEBREWS

EPISTLE

While classified as a letter, this book is more like a sermon that encourages people to remain firm in their hope of salvation and follow in the way of Christ. The readers (probably Gentile Christians) have faced persecution and are urged to keep the faith. The book demonstrates the superiority of Jesus Christ to the angels (1), the superiority of Christ's priesthood to Moses and the prophets (3–8), and the superiority of Christ's sacrifice to temple ritual (9–10). Christ, the great high priest, mediated a new covenant and offered the only really effective sacrifice. Christians were to be "pilgrim people" following in "the new and living way" given by Christ. This book persuasively argues that through Christ the faithful have direct access to God.

Outline

Christ over the angels (1); Christ's suffering (2); Christ over Moses (3:1–6); danger of unbelief (3:7–4:13); Christ, the great high priest (4:14–8:13); the worthiness of the sacrifice offered by Christ (9–10:18); exhortations to live as God's pilgrim people (10:19–13:17).

Famous Passages

The word of God is living, active . . . able to judge thoughts, intentions of the heart—4:12–13

We have a great high priest, Christ, who has been tested as we are, yet without sin—4:14–16

Christ is the mediator of a better covenant, enacted through better promises—8:6

Christ's death redeems us from transgressions under the first
　　covenant—9:15
Christ offered for all time a single sacrifice for sins—10:12–14
Faith is assurance of things hoped for, the conviction of things not
　　seen—11:1
Surrounded by great cloud of witnesses, lay aside sin, run the race,
　　look to Jesus—12:1–2
Do not neglect to show hospitality to strangers; may entertain
　　angels—13:2

JAMES

EPISTLE

James is not really a letter but rather a collection of teachings that tell Christians how to behave. It makes the point that one's faith needs to be expressed by what one does. This is to balance people who took too literally Paul's argument that it is faith, not works, that saves us. The writer also urges readers to reach out to the poor and avoid catering to the wealthy.

Outline

Faith under trial (1); love of neighbor (2); taming the tongue
　　(3:1–12); the perils of envy (3:13–4:12); the seductiveness of
　　wealth (4:13–5:6); patience and the power of prayer (5:7–20).

Famous Passages

Be quick to listen, slow to speak, slow to anger—1:19–20
Be doers of the word, not merely hearers—1:22
Faith without works is dead—2:14–26
The tongue is a fire—3:6a

Draw near to God, and he will draw near to you—4:8

Do not speak evil against one another—4:11–12

Suffering? Sick? Call the elders of the church for prayer, anointing with oil—5:12–14

The prayer of the righteous is powerful and effective—5:16

✤ ✤ ✤

1 AND 2 PETER

EPISTLE TO CHRISTIANS IN ASIA MINOR

1 Peter encourages Christians to have faith, imitate Christ, do good, endure any sufferings for their faith that come their way, and resist retaliating against those who speak against them. It may be a letter or come from liturgical material (prayers and sermons used in a baptism service, for example). Scholars vary in their assessment of genre, authorship, and dates, which range from 64–117 CE.

2 Peter is written as Peter's testament (a summary of his teachings to be passed on after his death). It urges readers to be ready for the day of the Lord's coming again. Most scholars believe it was written after Peter's death and ascribed to him, perhaps by an author from the church in Rome where Peter was a leader. It serves to restate and clarify Peter's teachings, especially for those who were criticizing his message of moral strictness in the context of a permissive society.

Outlines

1 PETER

Thanks for a new birth (1:1–10); living out a Christian's calling (1:11–2:11); Christian behavior at home and in community (2:11–3:22); final testing (4); the Christian community (5).

2 PETER

Living in the last days (1); God's judgment on false teaching (2); preparing for the end times (3).

Famous Passages

1 PETER

The resurrection of Christ gave us new birth into a living hope—1:2

You are a chosen race, a royal priesthood; once no people, now God's people—2:9–10

Do not repay wrong with wrong; respond with blessing—3:8–9

Maintain your love for one another; love cancels a host of sins—4:8

2 PETER

Look forward to the coming day of God . . . when justice will be established—3:12–13

✳ ✳ ✳

1, 2, AND 3 JOHN

EPISTLE

The first Epistle of John probably was a sermon or treatise written by someone from the same "school" as the writer of the Gospel by this name. It was written to counter those who denied the reality of Christ's incarnation and who claimed a superiority over others. It clarifies the faith around three themes: God is "light," God is "righteous," and God is "love."

2 John is a brief letter that urges mutual love and warns the church against offering hospitality to heretics.

3 John is a short letter written to an individual leader of a congregation who rejects the authority of the writer.

The writer's delegation had been turned away by another church leader. This letter tries to reestablish the writer's authority and asks the recipient to provide hospitality to the delegation.

Outline

See descriptions above.

Famous Passages

1 JOHN

If we claim to be sinless, we deceive ourselves and truth is not in us—1:6
If we confess our sins, he will forgive and cleanse us—1:9
God is love; he who dwells in love is in God and God is in him—4:16
Perfect love casts out fear—4:18
We love because he loves us first—4:19
God has given us eternal life, and this life is found in his Son—5:11–12

2 JOHN

What love means is to live according to the commands of God—6

3 JOHN

Do not imitate evil but imitate good—11

JUDE

EPISTLE

This brief letter is an urgent plea to all Christians to defend the faith against false teaching. Some people were destroying the Christian community by practicing immoral acts, apparently claiming that God's grace allowed them to do so with no concern for judgment.

Outline

See description above.

Famous Passages

Make your most sacred faith the foundation of your lives; pray in power of the Spirit—20

REVELATION

APOCALYPTIC LITERATURE

This book, written to a church under persecution, encourages Christians to keep faith. It may have been written during Nero's persecution of the Christians around Rome in 64 CE or during the persecution of Christians in the entire Asia Minor region that occurred under Domitian's reign (81–96 CE). The purpose of Revelation is to show that God, not Satan or any emperor, is Lord of history and that the faithful will be rewarded in the end.

Revelation is an example of apocalyptic literature in which an author relates a message from otherworldly beings (the Greek word *apokalypis* means "revelation"). These messages often are visions about the future. Like many Jewish apocalypses, Revelation uses a great deal of symbolism that can be very confusing. Because of this, Revelation is quite difficult to understand without considerable biblical knowledge and a good commentary to guide the reader.

Outline

Introduction, John's vision and commission (1); letters to the seven churches (2–3); vision of heaven (4–5); opening of the seven seals (6–11); seven visions (12–14); seven bowls of God's wrath (15–16:18); destruction of Babylon (16:19–19:10); Christ over the beast and the last judgment (19:11–20:15); the new heaven and new earth (21–22).

Famous Passages

I am the Alpha and the Omega; the beginning and the end—1:8, 21:6, 22:13

I wish you were either cold or hot . . . but lukewarm, I spit you out—3:16

Holy, holy, holy is God . . . who was, and is, and is to come—4:8

You are worthy to receive glory, honor, power; you created all things—4:11

Never again shall they feel hunger, thirst; God will wipe every tear from their eyes—7:16–17

I saw a new heaven and a new earth; the Holy City, the new Jerusalem—21:1

An end to death, mourning, crying, pain; the old order has passed away—21:4

The great street of the city was of pure gold, like translucent glass—21:15–21

The leaves of the trees are for the healing of the nations—22:1–2

SECTION

III

FURTHERING
YOUR
UNDERSTANDING

MAKING SENSE OF THE BIBLE

While the Bible can seem intimidating, there are a number of ways to make it easier to understand.

First, you will need a Bible! Don't necessarily use the "family Bible" in the living room that someone special may have given to you. A Study Bible with footnotes and an introduction to each book of the Bible is best.

While not necessary, you may also want to obtain a commentary (a book in which scholars explain each verse), a Bible dictionary, and a concordance (a list of key words and all the verses that contain each word). See "Tools for Further Study" (p. 282) for suggestions. Some Bibles will have brief dictionaries, maps, and other helps in the back of the book. This guide has a glossary and maps as well (pp. 263–81 and 300–9).

If you've never read the Bible or studied Scripture before, don't worry. You do not need any experience or special knowledge to read and enjoy the Bible. See if any of these suggestions appeals as a way of getting started:

1. Don't feel obligated to start at the beginning, with Genesis. Start with what attracts you. If you are looking for guidance or help from the Bible, try some of the passages listed under "Finding Help in the Bible" (p. 177). Read them. See if they "speak" to you. If not, try a favorite

Bible story you may remember ("Books of the Bible," p. 10).

Look around until you find the passages that "connect" with you. Try some of the methods described for individuals. The section on "Your Personality and Scripture" (p. 173) may help you figure out what passages and methods best match who you are. Or just pick up the Bible and read without any specific method or purpose in mind. Take days, weeks, or months. Don't set up any specific expectations for yourself. Just explore. Come back to explore again and see what else you can find. You're just getting acquainted now.

2. After a while, you will probably find several passages that speak powerfully to you. You may begin to realize that many passages seem to have several layers of meaning. And you would like to begin to look deeper.

Now is the time to find a couple of fellow travelers. If you haven't been to church or synagogue and are not comfortable with organized religion or "religious" people, pick a friend (or two) who also isn't "into religion" or whom you can trust not to "push" religion on you. You don't have to meet in a religious space or attend class. Just get together with friends to read the Bible and talk about what it means to you. Explore at your own pace and in your own way.

You might want to try out some of the methods in the book and see if they are helpful. Many people find the "Personal Response Approach" (p. 160) a good one to start with. If set "methods" don't appeal to you, just read and talk about the passages you select; try a short book like the Gospel of Mark or the Exodus story. Or use the lessons given for the week in the Complete Revised Common Lectionary (p. 193).

The further you go on this journey, the more important it becomes for you to walk alongside others traveling this same way.

3. At the point that you and your friends have ques-

tions you cannot answer, it is time, if you have not already done so, to look for a local church or religious group. If you really want to understand who God is, you need to explore your questions with Christians, Jews, or other people of faith. The understanding, knowledge, and experience of other seekers today and in the past will help you find your way to deeper spiritual development.

If you don't belong to a church or synagogue, look for one nearby to visit, alone or with a friend. Make an appointment to talk with the clergyperson or rabbi and tell him or her about what you hope to find. If the first one or two congregations don't feel right, keep looking. Churches and synagogues are very different from each other, and somewhere you are bound to find one that fits you.

If you are not growing spiritually, not learning more about yourself and God, talk with a clergyperson or experienced lay person of the congregation to see if the block is something in your life or in the congregation. If such people are not available or if the congregation is not able to help you, find another church or synagogue. Your spiritual growth is important, and you will be able to live a more full Christian or Jewish life if you are in a religious community where you are learning and growing.

Eventually, you will discover that your life has changed: people, goals, values, and your inner life will all seem different. Some of those changes may be small and subtle, some major. But as you draw closer to God, things will be different. When that happens, most people discover that the Bible has become a friend and companion they cannot live without. They are nourished by it, they live its truth, and their lives proclaim that truth to others. This can be a time of deep peace and joy.

Your journey may be very different from the one described here. Much depends on who you are, where you have been, and where you are going. The point is that there are no absolutely "right" ways to read or study the Bible.

If you are new to the Bible, take your Bible with the *Doubleday Pocket Bible Guide* in hand and begin to explore. If you have read the Bible from time to time, now is a perfect time to dig deeper.

Bible Editions Supply Built-in Helps

Some versions of the Bible, especially those called "study Bibles," will give an introduction to each book. The introduction will usually tell you something about the author, when and to whom the book was written, and what the book contains. An outline of the contents may also be provided.

Remember that all of this was added by the translators or publishers. And because scholars are still learning about the Bible, you may find differences between older Bibles and more recent ones. In addition, scholars often disagree about things like the date a book was written. Some of the Bible's books give good clues to their dates, others require us to make an educated guess using references to historical events documented in secular histories or using language peculiar to a specific time in history. Given these clues, different scholars understandably come to different conclusions.

It is often helpful to read different introductions to compare them. You should do the same thing with the descriptions offered in this book, as they come from several sources and offer the author's own perspective. You will need to do your own research and form your own ideas.

In addition to the material specific to each book, some versions of the Bible include articles about the entire Hebrew Bible or New Testament, the way people lived at various points in history, how the Bible was written, edited, translated and canonized, and so on. These articles can be very helpful in developing an understanding of the "big picture."

Notes and Cross-References

Your Bible may have a number of tiny numbers or letters scattered through the text and notes. They may appear below or within columns alongside the main text. The numbers (or letters) have a corresponding number somewhere on that page followed by a word, phrase, or explanation. These are notes that have been added by people much later, often in the past few years. They give a variety of information.

Some notes tell you something about how a word or phrase was translated, especially if there is any confusion about what was meant. Some notes explain something that may not be clear from the text or requires additional information to understand. Some provide cross-references that connect one verse with another verse somewhere else in the Bible that is related to or the same as the first verse. For example, in Mark 2:1–12, the story of the healing of a paralytic, a cross-reference to Matthew 9:1–8 and Luke 5:12–16 indicates that the same story is found in those two Gospels.

Again, these notes and cross-references can be confusing, so feel free to skip over them. But if you want to explore deeper, they give a quick and handy way to find alternative wordings, additional information, or references to related verses. The trick is to avoid getting distracted or turned off by the bafflement they might create in a new reader. The Bible itself is the main material to pay attention to!

Red Letters and Quotes

Somewhere around the turn of this century a printer got the idea of putting the words Jesus said into red print to highlight them. The idea caught on and for many years it was standard in most Bibles. Recently, it has started to die out again. This does not make the red-letter Bibles any more holy or better—just different!

By the same token, some printers put quotes in the New Testament from the Hebrew Bible into a form that makes them immediately recognizable. They may appear in block capitals or italics, for example. Again, this is just to make it easier for you to see them.

Maps, Glossaries, Lists

At the back of the Bible you may find a variety of other information. Maps are sometimes included, definitions of words, lists of various topics, or short concordances (word lists), which give an alphabetical index of key words and where they can be found.

Unfamiliar Words, Names, Places

As you read, you will find a lot of words, phrases, names, and places that you've never heard of. Sometimes it can be pretty daunting—especially if you try reading one of those long lists of unpronounceable names! It is best to skip over those parts initially unless you're intrigued by them and want to look for them in a Bible dictionary. And if you are reading aloud in a group or want to refer to one of those unpronounceable words, just take a crack at it! Some of them no one really knows how to pronounce. Some you can look up in a Bible dictionary and figure out. But mispronouncing a word is less important than getting to the heart of the passage. So read to get the sense of the story and don't worry too much about all those strange names and words.

There are thousands of people and places mentioned in the Bible, but only some of them stand out in the overall story. The Hebrew Bible was written for the people of Israel and the writer assumed they knew things we cannot know. Some of it has been pieced together by scholars, but some of it has been lost in the sands of history. So don't struggle trying to understand all those names and places. Get the important ones in place and let the others come later.

Finally, remember this story was originally told, not written. And it was told over and over for hundreds, even thousands of years. Some of the ways the people then saw the world are quite different from ours (the belief, for example, in a three-layered universe—the world was a flat plate with sky and heaven above that). Don't try to force ancient words and concepts into our modern language and way of seeing reality. Accept the story as told and seek to understand its meaning for you today.

Read the Bible Aloud

Because the Bible was originally passed along through storytelling, often the best way to understand it is to read it aloud. Because it was written more for the ear than for the eye, sometimes what you read will make more sense if you can hear it. This was very true in the original language, but it still is evident in the translations. So, when all else fails, try reading it aloud!

> [The Jews in Beroea] welcomed the message very eagerly and examined the scriptures every day to see whether these things were so.
>
> Acts 17:11b

There are many ways to read and study the Bible. This section will introduce several. It may be helpful at the outset, however, to break down what happens when we study the Bible in meaningful ways.

- *We formulate our understanding of the passage* by listening to it as a whole and in parts; identifying key words or phrases; researching who wrote it; examining to whom it was written, when, where, and why; exploring the writing style and what it tells us about the passage; identifying other passages that are similar or related; and asking what it says to us personally.

- *We connect it to our community* by asking how others responded to the passage and identifying how it relates to our lives and the issues faced by our neighbors, community, and the world. We also ask how we work together on the issues raised in the passage and look at how it calls us into community.

- *We act on it* by asking ourselves if we need to change direction in our lives, by identifying what we are called to do—as individuals or members of a group, and by naming the steps we need to take to create the change.

You can study the Scriptures alone or in a group. But because the Scriptures were developed in community and one of the Bible's major themes is God calling us into community, it is important that we regularly engage Scripture in community rather than just alone.

Selecting a Passage or Course of Study

There are many ways to decide what to read or study. Each has its strengths and weaknesses. Select the way that appeals to you. You can:

- read through a book of the Bible, studying a few verses at a time. If you are just starting, select an interesting book. One of the four Gospels (Matthew, Mark, Luke, or John) is a good place for Christians to start. In the Hebrew (Old) Testament, Genesis talks about the earliest stories of God's relationship with us, and Exodus tells one of the most important stories of God's calling of the Hebrew people.
- pick a topic and study passages about it. A concordance (which lists verses by key words) can help, and most Bible computer software programs let you search for key words. See "Finding Help in the Bible" (pp. 177–89) and "Aids to Study" (pp. 193–290).
- follow a lectionary, a set of passages assigned for a given day or week. This book contains a lectionary common to many Christian churches that you can use.
- study parts of the worship service based on the Bible or found in the Bible: the Psalms, the Shema, the Lord's Prayer, the Nicene Creed, hymns (songs), and prayers.

Before You Dig In

Set aside a specific time each day to read your Bible. Most people do best when they use the same time each day. Be realistic and honest about how much time you can expect to spend. Pick a time that fits your lifestyle, living situation, and personality rather than setting expectations for yourself based on what someone else does or what you think you "ought" to do. Do what works for you.

Find a comfortable place where you will not be distracted or disturbed. Some people find it helpful to use a desk to create a study mood. Others prefer a comfortable chair or even their bed.

Begin by meditating and praying for God's guidance and blessing. Slow down. Close your eyes. Take several deep breaths. Listen to the sounds around you. Become aware of God's presence. Create a space for you and God to spend time together.

A Guide to Three Approaches

What follows may help your study of the Bible become even more meaningful. While you will want to read and study the Bible in a way that best fits you, also try different approaches so you can see Scripture in new ways. While designed for specific settings, to some extent these approaches can be used interchangeably. They can help you or your faith community:

- learn about what the Scripture passage meant to people who first heard it
- hear what God is saying to you through the words in the Bible
- make decisions
- feel emotions and relate them to God
- live more holy lives

Note the three approaches to Scripture study that follow:

- Individual Approaches to Scripture
- Family Approaches to Scripture
- Group Approaches to Scripture

Individual Approaches to Scripture

Reading the Scriptures alone can be a meditative prayer experience as well as a time of learning. In addition to the suggestions, most of the group approaches described in this book also can be adapted to individual use.

> *Blessed are you, O LORD;*
> *teach me your statutes.*
> *With my lips I declare*
> *all the ordinances of your mouth.*
> *I delight in the way of your decrees*
> *as much as in all riches.*
> *I will meditate on your precepts,*
> *and fix my eyes on your ways*
> *I will delight in your statutes;*
> *I will not forget your word.*
>
> Psalm 119:12–16

A few simple suggestions:

- Write in a journal what you have thought, felt, or learned while reading; what you have discovered in commentaries or answers to discussion questions in the approaches described in this book.
- Respond artistically: draw, paint, write poetry, compose songs, or the like.
- Read the passage aloud even if you are alone. You will be surprised how different the passage becomes when it enters through the ear rather than just through the eye.
- Read, read, read. After reading the passage aloud, read what a commentary has to say about it. Then read the passage again. What in your understanding changed? What did you discover?

- Read a book in its entirety; some of the shorter epistles and the Gospel of Mark are especially good.
- Memorize a verse and repeat it to yourself throughout the day.
- Build on other experiences such as TV or radio broadcasts of religious worship services, video or TV programs on religious or social concerns, daily devotional booklets, and other reading material.
- Connect with others by writing letters to a Bible study pen pal or by signing on to a computer network and finding a person or group interested in reading and commenting on a passage.
- Write a book or series of talks for yourself or others.

MEDITATIVE APPROACH

PURPOSE: **To help individuals pray with the Scriptures**

NEEDED: **Relative quiet and undisturbed time and space**

BEST FOR: **Those inclined toward meditation, quiet, reflection**

Prepare in silence, becoming aware of God's presence.

Read the whole passage aloud, slowly and prayerfully.

Reflect on it as a whole. Do not focus on anything in particular. Close your eyes and let the words echo in your mind. See what emerges.

Read the passage aloud, paragraph by paragraph. Stop and reflect on each paragraph as you finish reading it.

Read the passage sentence by sentence. Stop and reflect on each sentence in turn.

Listen for what God may be saying to you through it.

Speak to God in your own words, saying what you heard and how it applies to your life.

CONVERSATIONAL APPROACH

PURPOSE: To help individuals use Scripture as an entry into prayer
NEEDED: Quiet, undisturbed time and space
BEST FOR: Those comfortable with imagination

Choose a passage where Jesus or God is speaking.

Prepare in silence, becoming aware of God's presence.

Read the passage aloud, slowly and prayerfully.

Close your eyes and picture where the story takes place; put yourself in the picture (as yourself, not as anyone else in the story).

Replay what Jesus or God said. Hear it as being said to you.

Begin a discussion with Jesus (or God) about what he has said; listen to how Jesus (or God) replies.

Carry on this conversation until it comes to a natural end.

Identify any dominant thoughts or feelings you had during the conversation. What might they tell you about your relationship with Jesus or God?

Thank God for what you have gained and ask for God's continued presence with you.

CONTEMPLATIVE APPROACH[1]

PURPOSE: **Help people use Scripture as a means of contemplative prayer**
NEEDED: **A Bible story and a quiet, undisturbed time and space**
BEST FOR: **Those inclined toward contemplative prayer**

Prepare in silence, becoming aware of God's presence.

Read the passage aloud, slowly and prayerfully.

Picture where the story takes place.

Ask for some grace, some gift related to the passage that you seek from God (more love for someone, greater understanding of a particular situation, etc.).

Imagine yourself as one of the people or as an object in the story and relive it, using all of your senses. (What do you see, hear, touch, smell, taste?)

What thoughts go through your mind? Feelings?

Rest silently in God's presence. Stay in the story without doing or saying anything. Just be in that place.

Speak to God/Jesus about your experience and how the passage applies to your life.

[1]The difference between meditation and contemplation is that meditation is reflecting on and thinking about a passage while contemplation uses the passage to help you just "be" in God's presence without so much thinking. Contemplation works well for some personality types and is next to impossible for others! So use the contemplative method only if it works for you.

Family Approaches to Scripture

> *Keep these words that I am commanding you today in your heart. Recite them to your children and talk about them when you are at home and when you are away, when you lie down and when you rise.*
>
> Deuteronomy 6:6–7

Families with children or teens, couples without children, or groups of people living in the same household (which may include a nursing home or other group setting) all have an opportunity to read and study the Bible together. Family groups composed of only adults can also use these approaches as well as those found under the section "Group Approaches to Scripture." Families with older children and youths can adapt some of the group approaches as well. Families with younger children will find the following approaches more useful.

Although children and youths will rarely if ever admit it, the effort to include them in reading and reflecting on Scripture is important for their growth. And their inclusion is important for the adults, who often gain from the insights of those who have not yet complicated and "covered up" Scripture in the way adults often do.

Most parents and other adults living with children and youths know them well enough to predict what will and will not work with them. Start with the approaches you anticipate will be most comfortable to the younger members of the family, asking the adults to adapt to their needs. Relax and make the experience enjoyable. Laughter, silliness, and fun are often the best aids to learning.

Older children and youths are often the most resistant to participating in any family activity, much less reading or studying the Bible. It may be helpful to ask them to select the passage, select the approach, and lead the family. Putting them in charge makes them less unwilling to do something they might not want to do. It also enables them to ask their questions or discuss their concerns indirectly by posing them in relationship to a Bible passage.

A ROLE-PLAYING APPROACH

PURPOSE: To help family members "feel" the story and relate it to their lives

NEEDED: A story with several roles; "playful" families

PROCESS: Reluctant children can be invited to assign roles to adults as a way to engage them. Encourage drama, be creative

BEST FOR: Families with young children

Read the passage.

Invite family members to volunteer for the different roles (if the story does not have enough parts, add bystanders or objects such as trees, buildings, the road, etc.)

Act out the passage.

Talk about: How did it feel? How did you feel about the other players? Does this remind you of a time or situation in your life? What did you learn?

Trade roles and repeat if you have time or desire to do so.

CRAZY-QUESTIONS APPROACH

PURPOSE: **To help families interpret and tell Bible stories**
NEEDED: **Pad and pen to write the questions**
PROCESS: **Let children take the lead in deciding whom to meet; write down all the crazy questions; make sure everyone helps develop the answers (avoid having adults "tell" the children the answers)**
BEST FOR: **Families with middle-school-age children**

Read the passage.

Ask the family to imagine they meet aliens from space, characters from a favorite TV cartoon show, animals that can talk, or other imaginative creatures. Decide who you will meet.

List all the questions you think your imaginative creatures would ask you about this passage, assuming they know nothing about the Bible. What would they find crazy, strange, or unusual about this passage?

Decide how you, as the only Christian or Jewish family left in the universe, will answer these questions and help your imaginative creatures come to know God (or Christ).

Talk about what you learned about the passage and how to tell others about it.

STORYTELLING APPROACH

PURPOSE: To help families apply biblical stories to their own lives

NEEDED: Bible stories (does not work with other types of passages)

PROCESS: It is important that adults and older youths get into the mood of "play" and story-telling

BEST FOR: Families with younger children and playful older youths and adults

Read the story. With younger children, discuss what happens in the story.

Invite family members to tell the story in their own words, using imagination and enthusiasm. Adults and youths can model this by being creative in their version—use common objects as props; use puppets, figurines, dolls; translate the story into everyday life and settings.

Discuss how the story "changed" as different people told it. Discuss what stayed the same.

Decide how each of you would act if you were each of the characters in a similar situation today.

Identify any similar situations in your life where this story might help you decide how to act.

AN APPROACH FOR WRITERS AND ARTISTS

PURPOSE: **To help families express their responses to Scripture through art and word**

NEEDED: **For writers: paper and pens. For artists: art supplies—colors, paper, glue, scissors, paints—whatever you can gather together.**

PROCESS: **Decide if you will be writers or artists or both; give everyone a stated amount of time to create; they can finish later if necessary. This exercise can be done over a week's time.**

BEST FOR: **Artistically inclined families and/or children; families with older children who enjoy writing**

Read the story or passage aloud.

Name aloud all the words that "jump out" at you (writers) or all the colors and images (artists) that come to your mind. Don't discuss them, just say them aloud.

Write a poem, song, story, letter; draw or build something that represents the passage to you.

Read what you have written or tell one another why or how your artistic creation represents the passage to you.

Listen to one another's readings and explanations; look at all the artistic creations.

Say what you learned about the passage, yourself, and God.

Group Approaches to Scripture

Small groups benefit from the different skills, experiences, and perspectives of their members. One person's strengths can balance another's weak points. Small groups also create accountability, keeping us from mistakenly going off on our own without anyone to challenge us or our interpretation.

> *Let the word of Christ dwell in you richly;*
> *teach and admonish one another in all wisdom;*
> *and with gratitude in your hearts sing*
> *psalms, hymns, and spiritual songs to God.*
>
> Colossians 3:16

Adults learn best when discovering a passage's meaning for themselves rather than having someone tell them what it means. The approaches described here assume that the group will do the work during the meeting with little or no prior preparation. The leader is primarily responsible for asking the questions, making sure everyone has a chance to respond, and then going to the next step.

These methods are designed to be led by inexperienced leaders. You do not have to know anything about the Bible or even have been a member of a small-group Bible study before. These methods can be used even by two or three friends who have never attended church or synagogue! If you have a larger membership you can rotate leading the group. See "Helps for Small-Group Leaders," page 170.

Four to eight members are the ideal size; the group meetings can extend indefinitely or for a specific period. An initial agreement to meet for six weeks usually is good for a new group. If you are starting a group, select people you know or with whom you are comfortable. It is better to recruit specific people than to issue a general invitation to a group (which often fails). Personal invitations make people feel wanted and are more likely to lead them to come. And don't forget that the best group for you might be your own circle of friends or a neighborhood group. This is especially true for those who may be uncomfortable with organized religion.

PERSONAL RESPONSE APPROACH

PURPOSE: To relate the passage to my life and hear God's word for me today

NEEDED: Three different translations of the Bible would be helpful but not necessary; pens and paper

PROCESS: Each person answers the questions in turn with no discussion or comment on what others say

GOOD FOR: People unfamiliar with the Bible; groups with different levels of experience. This approach can be done orally so is good with groups with those unable to read. (The steps that call for people to write their response can be omitted.)

Read the passage aloud.

Write the word or phrase that stands out for you.

Say the word or phrase that stands out for you.

Read the passage again (different reader).

Write: What did this passage mean to the hearers then, and what does it mean to me and my community now?

Say what you have written.

Read the passage again (different reader).

Write: What do I feel God wants me and my community to do in response? This week?

Pray aloud for the person on your right, including what they have said.

Note: After you have used this method several times, invite the group to discuss if they want time to write before speaking. The writing time greatly benefits those who need reflection time, but if your group does not have people with this need you can eliminate the writing time. Since this will change the nature of the group, you may want to reintroduce the writing step occasionally. Many groups move this into a discussion format, which is a different approach. The distinctive nature of this approach is that people respond *without* reacting to each other's comments (i.e. *not* discussing the passage). This sharpens one's listening skills and fosters a different perspective on the passage.

A modification on this approach: Use the same process but after the second reading invite people to identify the passage's themes and concerns. Then after the third reading listen for insights and challenges as they relate to issues they are dealing with in their lives, individually and communally.[2]

---

[2]This and variations of several of the following approaches were included in *In Dialogue with Scripture: An Episcopal Guide to Studying the Bible,* Linda L. Grenz, editor; Episcopal Church, 1995. All the approaches in this section are generally used in many churches and small groups and were not "invented" by me. You can create your own approach by mixing parts of these approaches and adding your own ideas.

AN ANALYTICAL APPROACH

PURPOSE: To learn facts about the passage that help you understand its meaning

NEEDED: Commentary or Bible with introductions to each book and many footnotes

PROCESS: Find answers to the first six questions; then discuss the "so what?" questions and plan a response

BEST FOR: People who want to know facts

Who is the audience? (recipients)

What was the author saying to them? (original message)

When was the passage written? (historical context)

Where was the author saying it? (social context)

Why was the author saying it? (purpose)

How did the author say it? (type of writing)

So what? What does it mean to me? (personal meaning)

What does it mean to us? (meaning for our community)

How do I or we respond? (plan for action or change)

SAY IT IN YOUR
OWN WORDS

PURPOSE: **To help people assimilate a passage in their own words and apply it to their lives**

NEEDED: **A passage with a story, interesting images, or action; pens and paper**

PROCESS: **Different people read the passage the first three times; each person reads his or her paraphrase; all discuss questions**

BEST FOR: **Those with little experience of the Bible; those who are creative, imaginative**

Read the passage aloud, emphasizing the nouns.

Read the passage aloud again, emphasizing the verbs.

Write the passage in your own words, using a modern setting if you like. Use story, poetry, song; write a letter, speech, or sermon.

Read your paraphrase.

Discuss what you learned from this passage.

Write the key actions from the passage in a column on the left side of the page.

Describe how you could apply each of the actions in your own life in a column to the right.

Discuss how you can apply what you learned to your life.

A THEOLOGICAL APPROACH

PURPOSE: To help people think about their relationship with God

NEEDED: A passage that shows the relationship between God and people; pens and paper

PROCESS: Different people read the passage; discuss
the questions; writing gives quieter people time
to gather their thoughts

BEST FOR: Groups with some experience in studying
Scripture

Read the passage.

Discuss what it tells us about God.

Read the passage again.

Discuss what it tells us about people.

Read the passage again.

Discuss what it tells us about the relationship between
God and people.

Discuss: How does this apply to my life, community,
and world? What does it tell me about my (our) relationship with God?

AN ELECTRONIC NETWORK APPROACH

PURPOSE: **To create worldwide study groups that provide broader perspectives on Scripture**

NEEDED: **Computer, modem, software, and access to electronic network**

PROCESS: **It is helpful to have one "coordinator" who keeps the conversation on track; post "norms" (rules for how you will function), update them, and remind participants of them regularly**

BEST FOR: **Computer buffs, those too busy to meet with others in person, or the homebound**

Sign on to an electronic network and create a bulletin board group, inviting others to join you in studying the Bible.

Post a passage (topical or from a lectionary) and a method (select from others in this book) and explain that each person will be invited to repond to one question each day, reading the others' responses as you proceed.

Invite group members to respond to the first question sometime during the first day.

Highlight the second question and invite people to respond to it the second day. Repeat for additional questions.

Add a final day to comment on one another's message to say what people learned before moving on to the next Scripture passage.

Encourage people to post prayer requests anytime.

AN EXPERIENCE-BASED APPROACH

> PURPOSE: To connect people's lives with Scripture and help them make decisions
>
> NEEDED: A concordance and preferably a set of commentaries
>
> PROCESS: Allow the presenter to describe the situation, but get the group to avoid focusing on it exclusively; use it to focus the group on the issue or question; avoid giving advice or solving the presenter's problem
>
> BEST FOR: A group with a high level of trust and considerable experience with the Bible and Bible tools

One group member describes a significant personal experience. It should be brief, unresolved, and (as much as possible) disguised or stripped of confidential material. (Do not tell tales on other people.)

Identify the key issues and questions in the experience. Each group member identifies a personal experience that raises similar issues or questions.

List Scripture passages that relate to the issues and questions identified (use a concordance).

Select four to five passages from your list to read and study.

Identify the key actions or messages in each passage. See if any patterns emerge. Identify passages that offer a different perspective.

Say what each of you has learned from your discussion and what choices or decisions, if any, you will make because of it.

Seek prayer support for any actions you intend to take. Agree on how and when you will report results back to the group.

A PRESENTATION APPROACH

PURPOSE: **To focus a group's attention on God's Word before or during a meeting or other program**[3]

NEEDED: **A leader prepared to make a presentation; questions written beforehand**

PROCESS: **Read, present, discuss for a couple of minutes, summarize; leadership can be rotated.**

BEST FOR: **Groups with limited time and another task**

Prepare a brief presentation beforehand; focus on one theme, issue, or question raised by the passage. Prepare one discussion question; write it so everyone can see it.

Invite a group member to read the passage.

Present your prepared talk.

Ask one discussion question; discuss as a whole group or in pairs for three to five minutes.

Summarize or ask participants to say what they learned to close the study time. If possible, connect to the meeting or program at hand.

Sample questions:

- How does this theme, passage, question relate to your life?
- When have you experienced this theme, question, issue?

[3]This approach was contributed by the Reverend Mark Anschutz.

- What do you find most difficult or most exciting about this?
- What one idea will you take home with you? What one thing did you learn from this passage?
- How does this passage affect our work/study in the rest of this meeting?
- What question or concern does this passage raise for you?
- How might we be called to change in response to this passage?

HELPS FOR SMALL-GROUP LEADERS

Before the Meeting

- Locate a comfortable meeting space that is relatively quiet and free from distractions. This can be a home, private dining room in a restaurant, or a meeting room in a church, synagogue, or community building. Nonreligious settings are often more comfortable for newcomers who are not members.
- Arrange comfortable chairs in a circle so everyone can see one another. Put your own chair in the circle so you can participate as well as lead.
- Provide name tags if people don't know one another.

During the Meeting

- Begin with a prayer, using a written prayer or one you offer spontaneously. Later you can invite others to offer the opening and closing prayers.
- Set goals by asking what people hope to gain from their time together. Write them so you can refer to them when you evaluate the group or if the group strays off into other areas.
- Agree on regular meeting times. Begin and end on time.
- Clarify group norms (ground rules for working together) before the first session and again whenever a new person joins. Decide on things such as smoking, consuming food/drinks, respecting one another's opinion, not pressuring one another to think or act in any specific way, taking turns, not dominating the discussion, and so on. It is helpful if the group adopts a

confidentiality norm that specifies that personal information not be discussed outside the group, unless it is clear that someone intends to harm themselves or someone else.

- Offer an approach or course of study or suggest several options.

- Explain the process of the approach you selected. This approach should be one you feel comfortable leading; later you can try others.

- Invite people to participate fully but give permission for anyone to "pass" on any question they may not have a response to or if they don't feel like sharing their response.

- Give people opportunities to participate by going around the group and inviting each person to respond before going to the next question. This is also a way to restrain those who tend to dominate. Remind dominators that they need to listen; encourage them to invite others to respond.

- Keep the participants on track by reminding them of the focus question or passage or by summarizing where they were before they went off track. If you are confused yourself, ask the group if this is what people want to discuss or if they are off track.

- Encourage everyone to help by listening to and supporting one another and by speaking for themselves (saying "I feel" rather than "We know that").

- Remind participants that differences are expected. The goal is to hear and learn from one another; not agree with one another or convince one another to adopt a certain viewpoint. The person most divergent from the rest of the group often provides the best opportunities for growth. Too much harmony usually eliminates growth.

- Pray about differences and learn from them rather than trying to resolve them, ignore them, or smooth them over.

- Value silence. Some people need silence to think. Their best contributions will emerge if they are given time and space to "mull." Those contributions are often the most profound.

- Provide a summary at the end; this helps the group see the ground they have covered.
- Invite people to say what they learned. This helps group members clearly identify and remember key things they learned.

After the Meeting

- Evaluate the group process with the group. Ask: How was this meeting for you? What would you like to do differently? What was especially good?
- Periodically do an in-depth assessment of your approach, topic, meeting time/space, and so on. Adjust accordingly. Occasionally include a written evaluation.
- Assess your role as leader. Ask yourself, How do I feel about my leadership? Ask the group, How do you feel about my leadership? Is there something I could do that would improve our meetings? Something I did you found especially helpful?
- Your role is to lead the group; you are not an expert on the Bible and you do not need to teach the group or give the answers. Your tasks are to handle the preparations, start and facilitate the meeting, and encourage group members to help one another.
- Group members are responsible for their own learning. Each person decides how he or she will participate and how much to choose to learn. If the group is not helpful, the individual is responsible for negotiating for changes or finding another group. You can help by asking group members if the group is meeting their needs. But if you start worrying about it between meetings, remind yourself that the group and each individual—not you—are ultimately responsible for the group's life.

YOUR
PERSONALITY
AND SCRIPTURE

W ho you are will affect how you respond to different passages or what reading and study approaches will work best for you. Different people will naturally prefer different approaches. It is important to recognize these differences so you will understand why one method or type of Scripture may be significant to you but less meaningful or frustrating to another person, or vice versa.

Some psychologists[4] say there are four basic pairs of words that can describe our personality. Each person uses both sides of each pair but most of us prefer one side over the other, much like being right- or left-handed. The combination of the four aspects creates sixteen different "personality types." Understanding these differences in how we process information and make decisions may help you in finding approaches to study—even Bible passages—that best fit who you are.

Are you more inward oriented or outward oriented?
If you are more inward oriented, you will tend to draw

[4]The Myers Briggs Type Indicator uses the terms Introvert/Extrovert, Sensing/Intuitive, Thinking/Feeling, and Judging/Perceiving. For more information see *Gifts Differing* by Isabel Briggs Myers, published by Consulting Psychologists Press, Inc., 1980, and *Please Understand Me* by David Keirsey and Marilyn Bates, distributed by Prometheus Nemesis Book Company, 1978.

energy from within yourself and like to go off alone to recharge yourself. You need time to reflect on Scripture; in group settings you may prefer writing out your thoughts before sharing them. You are likely to be comfortable studying alone. You may say less in a group, but what you say can be profound. People with this preference often like poetry, wisdom literature, and passages with many levels of meaning; they see those deeper levels while others are focusing on the story line.

If you are more outward oriented you will tend to draw energy from others and recharge yourself by meeting with friends, going out, or calling someone on the phone to talk. You tend to prefer studying in groups, "think on your feet," and learn by talking with others. You often lose interest when you study alone or when the passage is too indirect (as with poetry, for example). You generally like stories and passages that have dialogue and action. You can often make connections between the passage and many aspects of daily life.

Are you more sense oriented or intuition oriented?

If you are more sense oriented (take in information through your senses), you notice small details and can carefully describe what you see, hear, smell, feel, and taste. You tend to prefer concrete passages to poetry and are likely to look for answers to the who, what, when, where, why, and how questions. You take the passage for what it says and get uncomfortable with much interpretation, especially if the details in the passage don't all fit together exactly. You are likely to be more interested in genealogies, history, and laws than intuitive people (see next paragraph). Sense-oriented people often maintain a daily discipline of studying a certain number of verses or chapters.

If you are more intuition oriented, you "know" something but often don't know how or why you know it—you intuit information. You like stories and passages that have several levels of meaning, can easily find modern-day connections, and enjoy interpreting what a passage means.

You tend to take Scripture as a jumping-off point that leads to other books, events, and ideas. You are bored by genealogies, history, and laws and can get tired of trying to learn all the details about a passage. Intuitive-oriented people often learn in spurts and so find a daily reading routine difficult; they invest great energy in study for a while and then leave it and return later.

Are you more feeling oriented or thinking oriented?

If you are more feeling oriented you value harmony above all else; you want people in a group to agree and will work to make that happen. You can easily put yourself into the story, identifying with the people and situations. Feeling-oriented people often emphasize the "sacrificial victim" theme and can feel uncomfortable when there is conflict in a passage, when a passage points out where we have "fallen short," or when the group disagrees on what a passage means. You may then sacrifice yourself by giving up your viewpoint or overidentifying with the "wrong" viewpoint.

If you are primarily thinking oriented you value what is just and fair. You see disagreement in a group as good, a way to figure out what is right. It is fine by you if the group never reaches agreement so long as they are engaged in a real search for the truth. Thinking-oriented people tend to talk about "being responsible"; they see God as making demands on us and see humans as stewards of God's creation. They like passages that tell about people who made the right choices despite pressures. Their focus on concepts sometimes results in their being seen as uncaring.

Are you more closure oriented or exploration oriented?

If you are closure oriented you want to bring closure to issues, to come to a decision. Once something has been decided, you do not like to reopen the question for additional discussion. You like to systematically analyze a passage, decide what information about it is available, and then decide what it means. You are uncomfortable with discussions that range far and wide or that return to the same question more than once. You prefer organized, clear passages that can be applied directly to a modern situation, like biblical commandments and rules for living that are clear and concrete. Closure-oriented people sometimes accept the expert's or leader's word without much thought or discussion. They are disciplined, start and end groups on time, and have a set agenda for the group.

If you are more exploration oriented you are always ready to look at the question again in a new and different way. You do not really like to end the discussion and are not likely to accept someone else's interpretation of a passage. You want to hear everyone's ideas and discuss them at length. You look for new information and make lots of connections to other information or situations. This search sometimes leads to your never deciding what a passage means or never applying it to your life. You like complex passages with many applications and think that just one interpretation of a passage is "oversimplifying." You look for other commandments, situations, and passages that give another perspective to the one being studied.

This is a very simple description of a complex theory, but it helps us see how our personality shapes how and what we learn from the Bible. If you find yourself bored or frustrated, check to see if you are trying to work with a passage that is difficult for your personality type. If your group members seem to see things very differently, remember that God has given us different personalities, and don't assume that others are being unreasonable or difficult.

The scriptures are like a precious jewel that sits in the middle of a circle of people. Each of us sees a different face or facet of the jewel, but none of us sees the whole jewel in all of its brilliance. We can learn more about the jewel by listening to what others see—and we can help them by describing what we see. Experts can tell us about another part of the jewel that is not visible to us. Together we can begin to learn more about the Bible's multifaceted beauty.

FINDING HELP
IN THE BIBLE

Addiction

Psalms 40:1–5, 11–17; 116:1–7
Proverbs 23:29–35
2 Corinthians 5:16–21
Ephesians 4:22–24

Anger

Proverbs 15:1
Matthew 5:21–24
Romans 12:17–21
Ephesians 4:26–32
James 1:19–21

Anxiety, Worries

Psalm 25
Matthew 6:24–34; 10:26–31
1 Peter 1:3–5; 5:7

NOTE: This section is adapted from "Special Readers Helps" in the *New American Standard Bible*, copyright © 1991, by the American Bible Society.

Birth or Adoption of a Child

Psalm 100
Proverbs 22:6
Luke 18:15–17
John 16:16–22

Caring for the Aged and Widowed

Genesis 47:1–12
Ruth 1
Proverbs 23:22
1 Timothy 5:3–8

Child Rearing

Proverbs 22:6
Ephesians 6:4
Colossians 3:21

College

Proverbs 2:18; 3:1–18; 4:1–27; 23:12
Romans 8:1–17
1 Corinthians 1:18–31

Controlling Your Tongue

Psalm 12; 19:14
Proverbs 11:13; 12:16; 14:29; 15:1, 18; 16:32; 19:11;
    26:20; 29:11, 22
2 Thessalonians 2:16, 17
James 3:1–12
Ephesians 4:26–27, 31; 6:4

Cults

Matthew 7:15–20
2 Peter 2

1 John 4:1–6
Jude

Death

Psalms 23; 63:1–8
John 6:35–40
Romans 8:18–39
1 Corinthians 15:35–37
2 Corinthians 5:1–10
2 Timothy 1:8–10

Death of a Loved One

Job 19:25–27
John 11:25–27
John 14:1–7
Romans 8:31–39, 14:7–9
1 Thessalonians 4:13–18

Depression

Psalms 16; 43; 130
Isaiah 61:1–4
Jeremiah 15:10–21
Lamentations 3:55–57
John 3:14–17
Ephesians 3:14–21

Difficult Decisions

1 Kings 3
Esther 4–7
Psalm 139
Daniel 2:14–23
Colossians 3:12–17

Disappointment

Psalms 55; 62:1–8
Jeremiah 20:7–18

Discouragement

Psalm 34
Isaiah 12:1–6
Romans 15:13
2 Corinthians 4:16–18
Philippians 4:10–13
Colossians 1:9–14
Hebrews 6:9–12

Divorce

Psalm 25
Matthew 19:1–9
Philippians 3:1–11

Doubts About God

Psalms 8; 146
Proverbs 30:5
Matthew 7:7–12
Luke 17:5, 6
John 20:24–31
Romans 4:13–25
Hebrews 11:1
1 John 5:13–15

Fear

Psalms 27; 91
Isaiah 41:5–13
Mark 4:35–41
Hebrews 13:5, 6
1 John 4:13–18

Forgiveness

Psalms 32:1–5; 51
Proverbs 28:13
Joel 2:12–17

Matthew 6:14–15
Luke 15
Philemon
Hebrews 4:14–16
1 John 1:5–10

Friendship

Proverbs 17:9, 17; 18:24
Luke 10:25–37
John 15:11–17
Romans 16:1, 2

Frustration

Job 21:1–16; 24:1–17; 36:1–26
Matthew 7:13, 14

Future, Worrying About the

Isaiah 35; 60
Jeremiah 29:10–14
1 Peter 1:3–5
Revelation 21:1–8

Gifts, Tithes, Offerings

Exodus 35:20–29
Malachi 3:6–12
Luke 21:1–4
Acts 2:43–47; 4:32–37
Romans 12:9–13
1 Corinthians 16:1–4
2 Corinthians 8:1–15
2 Corinthians 9:6–15

God's Will

Psalm 15
Micah 6:6–8

Matthew 5:14–16
Luke 9:21–27
Romans 13:8–14
2 Peter 1:3–9
1 John 4:7–21

Graduation

Psalm 119:105–6
Proverbs 9:10–12
Galatians 5:16–26
Philippians 4:4–9

Growing Old, Worrying About

Psalm 37:23–29
Isaiah 46:3, 4

Help from God

Psalms 5; 57; 86; 119:169–176; 121; 130
Matthew 7:7–12

Homelessness

Psalm 90:1, 2
Isaiah 65:17–25
Lamentations 3:19–24
Luke 9:57–62
Revelation 21:1–4

Impatience

Psalms 13; 37:1–7; 40:1–5
Ecclesiastes 3:1–15
Lamentations 3:25–33
Hebrews 6:13–20
James 5:7–11

Imprisonment

Lamentations 3:34–36
Matthew 25:31–46
Luke 4:16–21

Inferiority, Feelings of

Isaiah 6:1–8
Jeremiah 1:4–10
Galatians 1:11–24
Ephesians 4:1–16
1 Peter 2:4–10

Insecurity, Lack of Confidence

Deuteronomy 31:1–8
Psalms 73:21–26; 108
Philippians 4:10–20
1 John 3:19–24

Jealousy

Psalm 49
Proverbs 23:17
James 3:13–18

Job, New

Proverbs 11:3; 22:29
Romans 12:3–11
1 Thessalonians 5:12–18
2 Thessalonians 3:6–13
1 Peter 4:7–11

Job Loss, Being Fired

Jeremiah 29:10–14
Luke 16:1–13
Philippians 4:10–13

Justice

Psalms 10; 17; 75; 94
Isaiah 42:1–7; 61:1–9
Amos 5:21–24
Habakkuk 1:1–2, 4

Leadership

Isaiah 11:1–9; 32:1–8
1 Timothy 3:1–7
2 Timothy 2:14–26
Titus 1:5–9
Romans 12:8

Life Alone

1 Corinthians 7:25–38; 12:1–31

Loneliness

Psalms 22; 42
John 14:15–31

Loss of Property and Possessions

Job 1:13–22; 42:7–17
Isaiah 30:19–26; 41:17–20
Romans 8:18–39

Marriage/Anniversary

Genesis 2:18–24
Song of Solomon 8:6, 7
Ephesians 5:21–33
Colossians 2:6, 7
1 Corinthians 13

Military Service

2 Samuel 22:2–51
Psalm 91
Ephesians 6:10–20
2 Timothy 2:1–13

Money, Worrying About

Proverbs 11:7
Ecclesiastes 5:10–20
Matthew 6:24–34
Luke 12:13–21
1 Timothy 6:6–10

Moving to a New Home

Psalm 127:1–2
Proverbs 24:3–4
John 14:1–7
Ephesians 3:14–21
Revelation 3:20–21

Natural Disasters

Genesis 8:1–9
Job 36:22–37
Psalms 29; 36:5–9; 124
Jeremiah 31:35–37
Romans 8:31–39
1 Peter 1:3–12

Peer Pressure

Proverbs 1:7–19
Romans 12:1, 2
Galatians 6:1–5
Ephesians 5:1–20

Persecution

Matthew 22:1–14; 25:1–13
2 Corinthians 12:1–10

Prejudice

Matthew 7:1–5
Acts 10:34–36
Galatians 3:26–29
Ephesians 4:11–22
Colossians 3:5–11
James 2:1–13

Pride

Psalm 131
Mark 9:33–37
Luke 14:7–11; 18:9–14; 22:24–27
Romans 12:14–16
1 Corinthians 1:18–31
2 Corinthians 12:1–10

Rejection

Psalm 38
Isaiah 52:13–53:12
Matthew 9:9–13
Luke 4:16–30
John 15:18–16:4
Ephesians 1:3–14
1 Peter 2:1–10

Relationship with God

Deuteronomy 5:1–22
Psalm 139
John 15:1–17
Romans 5:1–11; 8:1–17

Relationships with Others

Deuteronomy 5:16–21
Proverbs 3:27–35
Matthew 18:15–17, 21–35
Romans 14:13–23; 15:1–6
Galatians 6:1–10
Colossians 3:12–17
1 John 4:7–12

Respecting Parents

Exodus 20:12
Proverbs 23:22
Ephesians 6:1–3
Colossians 3:20

Retiring from Your Job

Numbers 6:24–26
Psalm 145
Matthew 25:31–46
Romans 12:1–2
Philippians 3:12–21
2 Peter 1:2

Salvation

John 3:1–21
Romans 1:16–17; 3:21–31; 5:1–11; 10:5–13
Ephesians 1:3–14; 2:1–10

Sexual Temptations

2 Samuel 11:1–12, 25
1 Corinthians 6:12–20
Galatians 5:16–26

Strength

Psalms 46; 138
Isaiah 40:27–31; 51:12–16

Ephesians 6:10–20
2 Thessalonians 2:16, 17

Stress, Feeling Overwhelmed

Isaiah 55:1–9
Matthew 11:25–30
John 4:1–30
2 Corinthians 6:3–10
Revelation 22:17

Suffering and Persecution

Psalm 109; 119:153–60
Matthew 5:3–12
John 15:18–16:4
Romans 8:18–30
2 Corinthians 4:1–15
Hebrews 12:1–11
1 Peter 4:12–19

Temper

Proverbs 14:17, 29; 15:18; 19:11; 29:22
Ecclesiastes 7:9
Galatians 5:16–26

Temptations

Psalms 19:12–14; 141
Luke 4:1–13
Hebrews 2:11–18; 4:14–16
James 1:12–18

Time Management

Proverbs 12:11; 28:19
Mark 13:32–37
Luke 21:34–36

1 Timothy 4:11–16
Titus 3:8–14

Tiredness, Weariness

Psalms 3:5, 6; 4:4–8
Isaiah 35:1–10
Matthew 11:25–30
2 Thessalonians 3:16
Hebrews 4:1–11

Trial or Lawsuit

Psalm 26
Isaiah 50:4–11
Matthew 5:25, 26
Luke 18:1–8

Truth

Psalm 119:153–160
John 8:31–47; 14:6–14; 16:4–15
1 Timothy 2:1–7

Vengefulness

Matthew 5:38–42
Romans 12:17–21

AIDS TO
STUDY

THE COMPLETE REVISED COMMON LECTIONARY

What Is a Lectionary?

It is simply a collection of passages (called readings or lessons) that have been compiled from Scripture for use in public worship or private devotions. The readings are put together either to reflect a theme (like the birth of Jesus at Christmas) or they provide for the reading of a large portion of one of the books of the Bible over a course of time (like the Acts of the Apostles during the Sundays following Easter). Lectionaries have been around a long time. Luke's Gospel speaks of Jesus standing in the synagogue and reading from the book of the prophet Isaiah, presumably the portion of text appointed to be read that day (Luke 4:14–21).

The Complete Revised Common Lectionary was developed by the Consultation on Common Texts, a group of Christian scholars appointed by their denominations to identify the wording for key liturgical texts (such as the Lord's Prayer) that could be used by all denominational groups. Since many of the lectionaries used by the denominations were quite similar, the group was in an ideal position to establish a common lectionary.

The Revised Common Lectionary is divided into three year-long cycles (Years A, B, and C). The lectionary is designed to provide over a three-year period for the reading of a great deal of the Old Testament (Hebrew Scriptures), all of the Psalms, and many selections from the Gospels and Epistles in the New Testament. (Once Year C is completed, the cycle begins again with Year A.) Each Sunday is assigned a reading from the Hebrew Scriptures, a Psalm, an Epistle selection, and a Gospel text.

The lectionary is based on the Christian church year (which begins on the First Sunday of Advent) and follows the general themes of the birth, death, resurrection of Jesus Christ; the coming of the Holy Spirit and the sending out of the disciples to preach the good news; and the teachings, healings, and miracles that Jesus performed in his earthly ministry. The great stories from the Old Testament are read alongside the Gospels, chosen to provide a thematic harmony. The Epistle lessons are also matched to the Gospel during the major seasons (Advent, Christmas, Epiphany, Lent, Easter, and Pentecost) but are read semicontinuously during the summer months of "Ordinary Time" so do not match the theme from the Hebrew Scriptures and Gospels. A selection from the Psalms that matches the theme of the first reading is included for each day.

The Revised Common Lectionary can be modified for use by any Christian group for devotional use and Bible study. Jews may wish to use a lectionary available from their synagogue or may choose to use just the selections from the Hebrew Bible.

The Complete Revised Common Lectionary
Developed by the Consultation on Common Texts

TITLES OF SUNDAYS AND SPECIAL DAYS

The following is a list of the Sundays and Special Days included in the Revised Common Lectionary.[1] The specific dates on which a given Sunday (such as the First Sunday of Advent) is observed changes from year to year. You can identify this year's dates by finding the calendar year below and then looking for today's date in that section. For a more detailed description of the Sundays and Special Days see pages 196–97.

YEAR A begins on the First Sunday of Advent in 1998, 2001, 2004, 2007, 2010. Year A begins on page 198.

YEAR B begins on the First Sunday of Advent in 1999, 2002, 2005, 2008, 2011. Year B begins on page 214.

YEAR C begins on the First Sunday of Advent in 1997, 2000, 2003, 2006, 2009. Year C begins on page 230.

1997	Year C	2002	Year B
1998	Year A	2003	Year C
1999	Year B	2004	Year A
2000	Year C	2005	Year B
2001	Year A	2006	Year C

[1]Each church may choose how to name each set of Sundays and Special Days, and whether or not to include all of these days in their own lectionaries.

Season of Advent

Four Sundays beginning with the First Sunday of Advent which is assigned to the Sunday between November 27 and December 3.

Season of Christmas

Begins with Christmas Day, December 25 through the Sunday prior to January 6.

Season of Epiphany

This season begins with the Epiphany (revealing) of the Lord, January 6 or the first Sunday in January until the last Sunday before Ash Wednesday (the beginning of Lent). Since Easter (which celebrates Jesus' resurrection) is a movable feast, it can occur as early as March 22 and as late as April 25. When Easter is early, it encroaches on the Sundays after the Epiphany, reducing their number, as necessary, from as many as nine to as few as four. In similar fashion, the date of Easter determines the number of Sunday Propers (set of lessons assigned to a specific day in the church year) after Pentecost. When Easter is as early as March 22, the numbered Proper for the Sunday following Trinity Sunday is Proper 3.

Season of Lent

Lent begins with Ash Wednesday and continues through Good Friday (the day of Jesus' crucifixion) and Holy Saturday (the day before Easter Sunday). Lent officially ends in the middle of the Easter Vigil service which waits for and then celebrates the resurrection of Christ.

Season of Easter

Easter begins in the middle of the Easter Vigil (usually observed on Saturday night or early on Easter Sunday) and continues to the Day of Pentecost.

Season After Pentecost (Ordinary Time)

The season begins on Trinity Sunday (the first Sunday after Pentecost) and continues through the summer and fall until the last Sunday before Advent (i.e. the Sunday between November 20 and November 26). These Sundays are assigned "Propers" which are numbered according to the usage by the Protestant and Episcopal churches in the United States.[2]

Special Days

February 2—Presentation of the Lord
March 25—Annunciation of the Lord
May 31—Visitation of Mary to Elizabeth
September 14—Holy Cross
November 1—All Saints
Fourth Thursday of November (United States), Second Monday of October (Canada)—Thanksgiving

[2]Propers are variable readings (or parts) of the mass or liturgy. Those numbered in brackets in the lectionary indicate the Proper numbering system of the Roman Catholic Church and the Anglican Church of Canada.

YEAR A

Begins on the First Sunday of Advent in 1998, 2001, 2004, 2007, 2010.

Season of Advent

FIRST SUNDAY OF ADVENT
Isaiah 2:1–5
Psalm 122
Romans 13:11–14
Matthew 24:36–44

SECOND SUNDAY OF ADVENT
Isaiah 11:1–10
Psalm 72:1–7, 18–19
Romans 15:4–13
Matthew 3:1–12

THIRD SUNDAY OF ADVENT
Isaiah 35:1–10
Psalm 146:5–10
James 5:7–10
Matthew 11:2–11 or Luke 1:47–55

FOURTH SUNDAY OF ADVENT
Isaiah 7:10–16
Psalm 80:1–7, 17–19
Romans 1:1–7
Matthew 1:18–25

Season of Christmas

Nativity of the Lord (Christmas Day)

Any of the following three Propers may be used on Christmas Eve/Day.

The readings from Propers II and III for Christmas may be used as alternatives for Christmas Day. If Proper III is not used on Christmas Day, it should be used at some service during the Christmas cycle because of the significance of John's prologue.

CHRISTMAS, PROPER I (A,B,C)

Isaiah 9:2–7
Psalm 96
Titus 2:11–14
Luke 2:1–14, (15–20)

CHRISTMAS, PROPER II (A,B,C)

Isaiah 62:6–12
Psalm 97
Titus 3:4–7
Luke 2:(1–7), 8–20

CHRISTMAS, PROPER III (A,B,C)

Isaiah 52:7–10
Psalm 98
Hebrews 1:1–4, (5–12)
John 1:1–14

FIRST SUNDAY AFTER CHRISTMAS
The following readings are used on the First Sunday after Christmas unless the readings for the Epiphany of the Lord are preferred.

Isaiah 63:7–9
Psalm 148
Hebrews 2:10–18
Matthew 2:13–23

JANUARY 1—HOLY NAME OF JESUS (MARY, MOTHER OF GOD) (A,B,C)

Numbers 6:22–27
Psalm 8
Galatians 4:4–7 or Philippians 2:5–11
Luke 2:15–21

JANUARY 1—WHEN OBSERVED AS NEW YEAR'S DAY
(A,B,C)

Ecclesiastes 3:1–13
Psalm 8
Revelation 21:1–6a
Matthew 25:31–46

SECOND SUNDAY AFTER CHRISTMAS DAY (A,B,C)

The following readings are provided for use when
Epiphany (January 6) is celebrated on a weekday following the Second Sunday after Christmas Day.

Jeremiah 31:7–14 or Sirach 24:1–12
  or Wisdom of Solomon 10:15–21
Psalm 147:12–20
Ephesians 1:3–14
John 1:(1–9), 10–18

Season of Epiphany (Ordinary Time)

EPIPHANY OF THE LORD (A,B,C)

Isaiah 60:1–6
Psalm 72:1–7, 10–14
Ephesians 3:1–12
Matthew 2:1–12

BAPTISM OF THE LORD [1] (FIRST SUNDAY AFTER THE
EPIPHANY)

Isaiah 42:1–9
Psalm 29
Acts 10:34–43
Matthew 3:13–17

SECOND SUNDAY AFTER THE EPIPHANY [2]

Isaiah 49:1–7
Psalm 40:1–11
1 Corinthians 1:1–9
John 1:29–42

THIRD SUNDAY AFTER THE EPIPHANY [3]

Isaiah 9:1–4
Psalm 27:1, 4–9

1 Corinthians 1:10–18
Matthew 4:12–23

FOURTH SUNDAY AFTER THE EPIPHANY [4]

Micah 6:1–8
Psalm 15
1 Corinthians 1:18–31
Matthew 5:1–12

FIFTH SUNDAY AFTER THE EPIPHANY [5]

Isaiah 58:1–9a, (9b–12)
Psalm 112:1–9 (10)
1 Corinthians 2:1–12, (13–16)
Matthew 5:13–20

SIXTH SUNDAY AFTER THE EPIPHANY [6]

Proper 1. If this is the Sunday before Ash Wednesday, this Proper may be replaced, in those churches using Transfiguration readings on this day, by the readings for the Last Sunday after the Epiphany.

Deuteronomy 30:15–20 or Sirach 15:15–20
Psalm 119:1–8
1 Corinthians 3:1–9
Matthew 5:21–37

SEVENTH SUNDAY AFTER THE EPIPHANY [7]

Proper 2. If this is the Sunday before Ash Wednesday, this Proper may be replaced, in those churches using Transfiguration readings on this day, by the readings for the Last Sunday after the Epiphany.

Leviticus 19:1–2, 9–18
Psalm 119:33–40
1 Corinthians 3:10–11, 16–23
Matthew 5:38–48

EIGHTH SUNDAY AFTER THE EPIPHANY [8]

Proper 3. If this is the Sunday before Ash Wednesday, this Proper may be replaced, in those churches using Transfiguration readings on this day, by the readings for the Last Sunday after the Epiphany.

Isaiah 49:8–16a
Psalm 131
1 Corinthians 4:1–5
Matthew 6:24–34

NINTH SUNDAY AFTER THE EPIPHANY [9]

Proper 4. The following readings are for churches whose calendar requires this Sunday, and do not observe the Last Sunday after the Epiphany as Transfiguration.

Deuteronomy 11:18–21, 26–28
Psalm 31:1–5, 19–24
Romans 1:16–17; 3:22b–28, (29–31)
Matthew 7:21–29

LAST SUNDAY AFTER THE EPIPHANY (TRANSFIGURATION SUNDAY)

The following readings are used in churches where the Last Sunday after the Epiphany is observed as Transfiguration Sunday.

Exodus 24:12–18
Psalm 2 or Psalm 99
2 Peter 1:16–21
Matthew 17:1–9

Season of Lent

ASH WEDNESDAY (A,B,C)

Joel 2:1–2, 12–17 or Isaiah 58:1–12
Psalm 51:1–17
2 Corinthians 5:20b–6:10
Matthew 6:1–6, 16–21

FIRST SUNDAY IN LENT

Genesis 2:15–17; 3:1–7
Psalm 32
Romans 5:12–19
Matthew 4:1–11

SECOND SUNDAY IN LENT

Genesis 12:1–4a
Psalm 121
Romans 4:1–5, 13–17
John 3:1–17 or Matthew 17:1–9

THIRD SUNDAY IN LENT

Exodus 17:1–7
Psalm 95
Romans 5:1–11
John 4:5–42

FOURTH SUNDAY IN LENT

1 Samuel 16:1–13
Psalm 23
Ephesians 5:8–14
John 9:1–41

FIFTH SUNDAY IN LENT

Ezekiel 37:1–14
Psalm 130
Romans 8:6–11
John 11:1–45

SIXTH SUNDAY IN LENT (PASSION SUNDAY or PALM SUNDAY)

Those who do not observe the procession with palms and do not wish to use the passion Gospel may substitute the Gospel and Psalm given for the Liturgy of the Passion with the Gospel and Psalm indicated for the Liturgy of the Palms. Whenever possible, the whole passion narrative should be read.

Liturgy of the Palms:
Matthew 21:1–11
Psalm 118:1–2, 19–29

Liturgy of the Passion:
Isaiah 50:4–9a
Psalm 31:9–16
Philippians 2:5–11
Matthew 26:14–27:66 or Matthew 27:11–54

Holy Week

MONDAY OF HOLY WEEK (A,B,C)

Isaiah 42:1–9
Psalm 36:5–11
Hebrews 9:11–15
John 12:1–11

TUESDAY OF HOLY WEEK (A,B,C)

Isaiah 49:1–7
Psalm 71:1–14
1 Corinthians 1:18–31
John 12:20–36

WEDNESDAY OF HOLY WEEK (A,B,C)

Isaiah 50:4–9a
Psalm 70
Hebrews 12:1–3
John 13:21–32

HOLY THURSDAY (A,B,C)

Exodus 12:1–4, (5–10), 11–14
Psalm 116:1–2, 12–19
1 Corinthians 11:23–26
John 13:1–17, 31b–35

GOOD FRIDAY (A,B,C)

Isaiah 52:13–53:12
Psalm 22
Hebrews 10:16–25 or Hebrews 4:14–16; 5:7–9
John 18:1–19:42

HOLY SATURDAY (A,B,C)

The following readings are for use at services other than the Easter Vigil.

Job 14:1–14 or Lamentations 3:1–9, 19–24
Psalm 31:1–4, 15–16
1 Peter 4:1–8
Matthew 27:57–66 or John 19:38–42

Season of Easter

RESURRECTION OF THE LORD, EASTER VIGIL (A,B,C)

The following readings and psalms are provided for use at the Easter Vigil. A minimum of three Old Testament readings should be chosen. The reading from Exodus 14 should always be used.

Old Testament Readings and Psalms (A,B,C):
Genesis 1:1–2:4a with Psalm 136:1–9, 23–26
Genesis 7:1–5, 11–18; 8:6–18; 9:8–13 with Psalm 46
Genesis 22:1–18 with Psalm 16
Exodus 14:10–31; 15:20–21 with Exodus 15:1b–13, 17–18
Isaiah 55:1–11 with Isaiah 12:2–6
Baruch 3:9–15, 32–4:4 or Proverbs 8:1–8, 19–21; 9:4b–6 with
    Psalm 19
Ezekiel 36:24–28 with Psalm 42 and 43
Ezekiel 37:1–14 with Psalm 143
Zephaniah 3:14–20 with Psalm 98

New Testament Reading (A,B,C):
Romans 6:3–11
Psalm 114
Gospel: Matthew 28:1–10

RESURRECTION OF THE LORD, EASTER DAY

First Reading: Acts 10:34–43 or Jeremiah 31:1–6
Psalm 118:1–2, 14–24
Second Reading: Colossians 3:1–4 or Acts 10:34–43
Gospel: John 20:1–18 or Matthew 28:1–10

EASTER EVENING (A,B,C)

The following readings are for occasions when the main (eucharistic) Easter service must be late in the day. They are not intended for Vespers (Evening Prayer) on Easter Evening.

Isaiah 25:6–9
Psalm 114
1 Corinthians 5:6b–8
Luke 24:13–49

SECOND SUNDAY OF EASTER

Acts 2:14a, 22–32
Psalm 16
1 Peter 1:3–9
John 20:19–31

THIRD SUNDAY OF EASTER

Acts 2:14a, 36–41
Psalm 116:1–4, 12–19
1 Peter 1:17–23
Luke 24:13–35

FOURTH SUNDAY OF EASTER

Acts 2:42–47
Psalm 23
1 Peter 2:19–25
John 10:1–10

FIFTH SUNDAY OF EASTER

Acts 7:55–60
Psalm 31:1–5, 15–16
1 Peter 2:2–10
John 14:1–14

SIXTH SUNDAY OF EASTER

Acts 17:22–31
Psalm 66:8–20
1 Peter 3:13–22
John 14:15–21

ASCENSION OF THE LORD (A,B,C)
    The following readings may also be used on the Seventh Sunday of Easter.

Acts 1:1–11
Psalm 47 or Psalm 93
Ephesians 1:15–23
Luke 24:44–53

SEVENTH SUNDAY OF EASTER

Acts 1:6–14
Psalm 68:1–10, 32–35

1 Peter 4:12–14; 5:6–11
John 17:1–11

DAY OF PENTECOST
If the passage from Numbers is chosen for the First Reading, the passage from Acts is used as the Second Reading.

First Reading: Acts 2:1–21 or Numbers 11:24–30
Psalm 104:24–34, 35b
Second Reading: 1 Corinthians 12:3b–13 or Acts 2:1–21
Gospel: John 20:19–23 or John 7:37–39

Season After Pentecost (Ordinary Time)

TRINITY SUNDAY (First Sunday after Pentecost)

Genesis 1:1–2:4a
Psalm 8
2 Corinthians 13:11–13
Matthew 28:16–20

If the Sunday between May 24 and 28 inclusive follows Trinity Sunday, the Proper for the Eighth Sunday after the Epiphany [8] is used.

PROPER 4 [9]

SUNDAY BETWEEN MAY 29 AND JUNE 4 INCLUSIVE (If after Trinity Sunday)

Genesis 6:9–22; 7:24; 8:14–19 with Psalm 46 or
Deuteronomy 11:18–21, 26–28 with Psalm 31:1–5, 19–24
Romans 1:16–17; 3:22b–28, (29–31)
Matthew 7:21–29

PROPER 5 [10]

SUNDAY BETWEEN JUNE 5 AND JUNE 11 INCLUSIVE (If after Trinity Sunday)

Genesis 12:1–9 with Psalm 33:1–12 or
Hosea 5:15–6:6 with Psalm 50:7–15

Romans 4:13–25
Matthew 9:9–13, 18–26

PROPER 6 [11]

SUNDAY BETWEEN JUNE 12 AND JUNE 18 INCLUSIVE (If after Trinity Sunday)

Genesis 18:1–15, (21:1–7) with Psalm 116:1–2, 12–19 or
Exodus 19:2–8a with Psalm 100
Romans 5:1–8
Matthew 9:35–10:8, (9–23)

PROPER 7 [12]

SUNDAY BETWEEN JUNE 19 AND JUNE 25 INCLUSIVE (If after Trinity Sunday)

Genesis 21:8–21 with Psalm 86:1–10, 16–17 or
Jeremiah 20:7–13 with Psalm 69:7–10, (11–15), 16–18
Romans 6:1b–11
Matthew 10:24–39

PROPER 8 [13]

SUNDAY BETWEEN JUNE 26 AND JULY 2 INCLUSIVE

Genesis 22:1–14 with Psalm 13 or
Jeremiah 28:5–9 with Psalm 89:1–4, 15–18
Romans 6:12–23
Matthew 10:40–42

PROPER 9 [14]

SUNDAY BETWEEN JULY 3 AND JULY 9 INCLUSIVE

Genesis 24:34–38, 42–49, 58–67 with Psalm 45:10–17 or
Zechariah 9:9–12 with Psalm 145:8–14
Song of Solomon 2:8–13
Romans 7:15–25a
Matthew 11:16–19, 25–30

PROPER 10 [15]

SUNDAY BETWEEN JULY 10 AND JULY 16 INCLUSIVE

Genesis 25:19–34 with Psalm 119:105–112 or
Isaiah 55:10–13 with Psalm 65:(1–8), 9–13

Romans 8:1–11
Matthew 13:1–9, 18–23

PROPER 11 [16]

SUNDAY BETWEEN JULY 17 AND JULY 23 INCLUSIVE

Genesis 28:10–19a with Psalm 139:1–12, 23–24 or
Wisdom of Solomon 12:13, 16–19 or Isaiah 44:6–8 with Psalm
    86:11–17
Romans 8:12–25
Matthew 13:24–30, 36–43

PROPER 12 [17]

SUNDAY BETWEEN JULY 24 AND JULY 30 INCLUSIVE

Genesis 29:15–28 with Psalm 105:1–11, 45b and Psalm 128 or
1 Kings 3:5–12 with Psalm 119:129–136
Romans 8:26–39
Matthew 13:31–33, 44–52

PROPER 13 [18]

SUNDAY BETWEEN JULY 31 AND AUGUST 6 INCLUSIVE

Genesis 32:22–31 with Psalm 17:1–7, 15 or
Isaiah 55:1–5 with Psalm 145:8–9, 14–21
Romans 9:1–5
Matthew 14:13–21

PROPER 14 [19]

SUNDAY BETWEEN AUGUST 7 AND AUGUST 13 INCLUSIVE

Genesis 37:1–4, 12–28 with Psalm 105:1–6, 16–22, 45b or
1 Kings 19:9–18 with Psalm 85:8–13
Romans 10:5–15
Matthew 14:22–33

PROPER 15 [20]

SUNDAY BETWEEN AUGUST 14 AND AUGUST 20
INCLUSIVE

Genesis 45:1–15 with Psalm 133 or
Isaiah 56:1, 6–8 with Psalm 67

Romans 11:1–2a, 29–32
Matthew 15:(10–20), 21–28

PROPER 16 [21]

SUNDAY BETWEEN AUGUST 21 AND AUGUST 27
INCLUSIVE

Exodus 1:8–2:10 with Psalm 124 or
Isaiah 51:1–6 with Psalm 138
Romans 12:1–8
Matthew 16:13–20

PROPER 17 [22]

SUNDAY BETWEEN AUGUST 28 AND SEPTEMBER 3
INCLUSIVE

Exodus 3:1–15 with Psalm 105:1–6, 23–26, 45c or
Jeremiah 15:15–21 with Psalm 26:1–8
Romans 12:9–21
Matthew 16:21–28

PROPER 18 [23]

SUNDAY BETWEEN SEPTEMBER 4 AND SEPTEMBER 10
INCLUSIVE

Exodus 12:1–14 with Psalm 149 or
Ezekiel 33:7–11 with Psalm 119:33–40
Romans 13:8–14
Matthew 18:15–20

PROPER 19 [24]

SUNDAY BETWEEN SEPTEMBER 11 AND SEPTEMBER 17
INCLUSIVE

Exodus 14:19–31 with Psalm 114 and Exodus 15:1b–11, 20–21
    or Genesis 50:15–21 with Psalm 103:(1–7), 8–13
Romans 14:1–12
Matthew 18:21–35

PROPER 20 [25]

SUNDAY BETWEEN SEPTEMBER 18 AND SEPTEMBER 24
INCLUSIVE

Exodus 16:2–15 with Psalm 105:1–6, 37–45 or
Jonah 3:10–4:11 with Psalm 145:1–8
Philippians 1:21–30
Matthew 20:1–16

PROPER 21 [26]

SUNDAY BETWEEN SEPTEMBER 25 AND OCTOBER 1
INCLUSIVE

Exodus 17:1–7 with Psalm 78:1–4, 12–16 or
Ezekiel 18:1–4, 25–32 with Psalm 25:1–9
Philippians 2:1–13
Matthew 21:23–32

PROPER 22 [27]

SUNDAY BETWEEN OCTOBER 2 AND OCTOBER 8
INCLUSIVE

Exodus 20:1–4, 7–9, 12–20 with Psalm 19 or
Isaiah 5:1–7 with Psalm 80:7–15
Philippians 3:4b–14
Matthew 21:33–46

PROPER 23 [28]

SUNDAY BETWEEN OCTOBER 9 AND OCTOBER 15
INCLUSIVE

Exodus 32:1–14 with Psalm 106:1–6, 19–23 or
Isaiah 25:1–9 with Psalm 23
Philippians 4:1–9
Matthew 22:1–14

PROPER 24 [29]

SUNDAY BETWEEN OCTOBER 16 AND OCTOBER 22
INCLUSIVE

Exodus 33:12–23 with Psalm 99 or
Isaiah 45:1–7 with Psalm 96:1–9, (10–13)

1 Thessalonians 1:1–10
Matthew 22:15–22

PROPER 25 [30]

SUNDAY BETWEEN OCTOBER 23 AND OCTOBER 29
INCLUSIVE

Deuteronomy 34:1–12 with Psalm 90:1–6, 13–17 or
Leviticus 19:1–2, 15–18 with Psalm 1
1 Thessalonians 2:1–8
Matthew 22:34–46

PROPER 26 [31]

SUNDAY BETWEEN OCTOBER 30 AND NOVEMBER 5
INCLUSIVE

Joshua 3:7–17 with Psalm 107:1–7, 33–37 or
Micah 3:5–12 with Psalm 43
1 Thessalonians 2:9–13
Matthew 23:1–12

PROPER 27 [32]

SUNDAY BETWEEN NOVEMBER 6 AND NOVEMBER 12
INCLUSIVE

Joshua 24:1–3a, 14–25 with Psalm 78:1–7 or
Wisdom of Solomon 6:12–16 or Amos 5:18–24 with Wisdom of
    Solomon 6:17–20 and Psalm 70
1 Thessalonians 4:13–18
Matthew 25:1–13

PROPER 28 [33]

SUNDAY BETWEEN NOVEMBER 13 AND NOVEMBER 19
INCLUSIVE

Judges 4:1–7 with Psalm 123 or
Zephaniah 1:7, 12–18 with Psalm 90:1–8, (9–11), 12
1 Thessalonians 5:1–11
Matthew 25:14–30

PROPER 29 [34] (Reign of Christ or Christ the King)

SUNDAY BETWEEN NOVEMBER 20 AND NOVEMBER 26
INCLUSIVE

Ezekiel 34:11–16, 20–24 with Psalm 95:1–7a or 100
Ephesians 1:15–23
Matthew 25:31–46

ALL SAINTS, NOVEMBER 1 OR THE FIRST SUNDAY IN
NOVEMBER

Revelation 7:9–17
Psalm 34:1–10, 22
1 John 3:1–3
Matthew 5:1–12

THANKSGIVING DAY (Fourth Thursday in November in the
United States; Second Monday in October in Canada)

Deuteronomy 8:7–18
Psalm 65
2 Corinthians 9:6–15
Luke 17:11–19

YEAR B

Begins on the First Sunday of Advent 1999, 2002, 2005, 2008, 2011.

Season of Advent

FIRST SUNDAY OF ADVENT

Isaiah 64:1–9
Psalm 80:1–7, 17–19
1 Corinthians 1:3–9
Mark 13:24–37

SECOND SUNDAY OF ADVENT

Isaiah 40:1–11
Psalm 85:1–2, 8–13
2 Peter 3:8–15a
Mark 1:1–8

THIRD SUNDAY OF ADVENT

Isaiah 61:1–4, 8–11
Psalm 126
1 Thessalonians 5:16–24
John 1:6–8, 19–28 or Luke 1:47–55

FOURTH SUNDAY OF ADVENT

2 Samuel 7:1–11, 16
Luke 1:47–55 or Psalm 89:1–4, 19–26
Romans 16:25–27
Luke 1:26–38

Season of Christmas

Nativity of the Lord (Christmas Day)

Any of the following three Propers may be used on Christmas Eve/Day.

The readings from Propers II and III for Christmas may be used as alternatives for Christmas Day. If Proper III is not used on Christmas Day, it should be used at some service during the Christmas cycle because of the significance of John's prologue.

CHRISTMAS, PROPER I (A,B,C)

Isaiah 9:2–7
Psalm 96
Titus 2:11–14
Luke 2:1–14, (15–20)

CHRISTMAS, PROPER II (A,B,C)

Isaiah 62:6–12
Psalm 97
Titus 3:4–7
Luke 2:(1–7), 8–20

CHRISTMAS, PROPER III (A,B,C)

Isaiah 52:7–10
Psalm 98
Hebrews 1:1–4, (5–12)
John 1:1–14

FIRST SUNDAY AFTER CHRISTMAS DAY
The following readings are used on the First Sunday after Christmas unless the readings for the Epiphany of the Lord are preferred.

Isaiah 61:10–62:3
Psalm 148
Galatians 4:4–7
Luke 2:22–40

JANUARY 1—HOLY NAME OF JESUS (MARY, MOTHER OF GOD) (A,B,C)

Numbers 6:22–27
Psalm 8
Galatians 4:4–7 or Philippians 2:5–11
Luke 2:15–21

JANUARY 1—WHEN OBSERVED AS NEW YEAR'S DAY
(A,B,C)

Ecclesiastes 3:1–13
Psalm 8
Revelation 21:1–6a
Matthew 25:31–46

SECOND SUNDAY AFTER CHRISTMAS DAY (A,B,C)

The following readings are provided for use when
Epiphany (January 6) is celebrated on a weekday following the Second Sunday after Christmas Day.

Jeremiah 31:7–14 or Sirach 24:1–12
Psalm 147:12–20 or Wisdom of Solomon 10:15–21
Ephesians 1:3–14
John 1:(1–9), 10–18

Season of Epiphany (Ordinary Time)

EPIPHANY OF THE LORD (A,B,C)

Isaiah 60:1–6
Psalm 72:1–7, 10–14
Ephesians 3:1–12
Matthew 2:1–12

BAPTISM OF THE LORD [1] (FIRST SUNDAY AFTER THE
EPIPHANY)

Genesis 1:1–5
Psalm 29
Acts 19:1–7
Mark 1:4–11

SECOND SUNDAY AFTER THE EPIPHANY [2]

1 Samuel 3:1–10, (11–20)
Psalm 139:1–6, 13–18
1 Corinthians 6:12–20
John 1:43–51

THIRD SUNDAY AFTER THE EPIPHANY [3]

Jonah 3:1–5, 10
Psalm 62:5–12

1 Corinthians 7:29–31
Mark 1:14–20

FOURTH SUNDAY AFTER THE EPIPHANY [4]

Deuteronomy 18:15–20
Psalm 111
1 Corinthians 8:1–13
Mark 1:21–28

FIFTH SUNDAY AFTER THE EPIPHANY [5]

Isaiah 40:21–31
Psalm 147:1–11, 20c
1 Corinthians 9:16–23
Mark 1:29–39

SIXTH SUNDAY AFTER THE EPIPHANY [6]

Proper 1. If this is the Sunday before Ash Wednesday, this Proper may be replaced, in churches using Transfiguration readings on this day, by the readings for the Last Sunday after the Epiphany.

2 Kings 5:1–14
Psalm 30
1 Corinthians 9:24–27
Mark 1:40–45

SEVENTH SUNDAY AFTER THE EPIPHANY [7]

Proper 2. If this is the Sunday before Ash Wednesday, this Proper may be replaced, in churches using Transfiguration readings on this day, by the readings for the Last Sunday after the Epiphany.

Isaiah 43:18–25
Psalm 41
2 Corinthians 1:18–22
Mark 2:1–12

EIGHTH SUNDAY AFTER THE EPIPHANY [8]

Proper 3. If this is the Sunday before Ash Wednesday, this Proper may be replaced, in those churches using Transfiguration readings on this day, by the readings for the Last Sunday after the Epiphany.

Hosea 2:14–20
Psalm 103:1–13, 22
2 Corinthians 3:1–6
Mark 2:13–22

NINTH SUNDAY AFTER THE EPIPHANY [9]

Proper 4. The following readings are for churches whose calendar requires this Sunday, and do not observe the Last Sunday after the Epiphany as Transfiguration.

Deuteronomy 5:12–15
Psalm 81:1–10
2 Corinthians 4:5–12
Mark 2:23–3:6

LAST SUNDAY AFTER THE EPIPHANY (TRANSFIGURATION SUNDAY)

The following readings are used in churches where the Last Sunday after the Epiphany is observed as Transfiguration Sunday.

2 Kings 2:1–12
Psalm 50:1–6
2 Corinthians 4:3–6
Mark 9:2–9

Season of Lent

ASH WEDNESDAY (A,B,C)

Joel 2:1–2, 12–17 or Isaiah 58:1–12
Psalm 51:1–17
2 Corinthians 5:20b–6:10
Matthew 6:1–6, 16–21

FIRST SUNDAY IN LENT

Genesis 9:8–17
Psalm 25:1–10
1 Peter 3:18–22
Mark 1:9–15

SECOND SUNDAY IN LENT

Genesis 17:1–7, 15–16
Psalm 22:23–31
Romans 4:13–25
Mark 8:31–38 or Mark 9:2–9

THIRD SUNDAY IN LENT

Exodus 20:1–17
Psalm 19
1 Corinthians 1:18–25
John 2:13–22

FOURTH SUNDAY IN LENT

Numbers 21:4–9
Psalm 107:1–3, 17–22
Ephesians 2:1–10
John 3:14–21

FIFTH SUNDAY IN LENT

Jeremiah 31:31–34
Psalm 51:1–12 or Psalm 119:9–16
Hebrews 5:5–10
John 12:20–33

SIXTH SUNDAY IN LENT (PASSION SUNDAY or PALM SUNDAY)

Those who do not observe the procession with palms and do not wish to use the passion Gospel may substitute the Gospel and Psalm given for the Liturgy of the Passion with the Gospel and Psalm indicated for the Liturgy of the Palms. Whenever possible, the whole passion narrative should be read.

Liturgy of the Palms:
Mark 11:1–11 or John 12:12–16
Psalm 118:1–2, 19–29

Liturgy of the Passion:
Isaiah 50:4–9a
Psalm 31:9–16
Philippians 2:5–11
Mark 14:1–15:47 or Mark 15:1–39, (40–47)

Holy Week

MONDAY OF HOLY WEEK (A,B,C)

Isaiah 42:1–9
Psalm 36:5–11
Hebrews 9:11–15
John 12:1–11

TUESDAY OF HOLY WEEK (A,B,C)

Isaiah 49:1–7
Psalm 71:1–14
1 Corinthians 1:18–31
John 12:20–36

WEDNESDAY OF HOLY WEEK (A,B,C)

Isaiah 50:4–9a
Psalm 70
Hebrews 12:1–3
John 13:21–32

HOLY THURSDAY (A,B,C)

Exodus 12:1–4, (5–10), 11–14
Psalm 116:1–2, 12–19
1 Corinthians 11:23–26
John 13:1–17, 31b–35

GOOD FRIDAY (A,B,C)

Isaiah 52:13–53:12
Psalm 22
Hebrews 10:16–25 or Hebrews 4:14–16; 5:7–9
John 18:1–19:42

HOLY SATURDAY (A,B,C)

The following readings are for use at services other than the Easter Vigil.

Job 14:1–14 or Lamentations 3:1–9, 19–24
Psalm 31:1–4, 15–16
1 Peter 4:1–8
Matthew 27:57–66 or John 19:38–42

Season of Easter

RESURRECTION OF THE LORD, EASTER VIGIL (A,B,C)

The following readings and psalms are provided for use at the Easter Vigil. A minimum of three Old Testament readings should be chosen. The reading from Exodus 14 should always be used.

Old Testament Readings and Psalms (A,B,C):
Genesis 1:1–2:4a with Psalm 136:1–9, 23–26
Genesis 7:1–5, 11–18; 8:6–18; 9:8–13 with Psalm 46
Genesis 22:1–18 with Psalm 16
Exodus 14:10–31; 15:20–21 with Exodus 15:1b–13, 17–18
Isaiah 55:1–11 with Isaiah 12:2–6
Baruch 3:9–15, 32–4:4 or Proverbs 8:1–8, 19–21; 9:4b–6 with
    Psalm 19
Ezekiel 36:24–28 with Psalm 42 and 43
Ezekiel 37:1–14 with Psalm 143
Zephaniah 3:14–20 with Psalm 98

New Testament Reading (A,B,C):
Romans 6:3–11
Psalm 114
Gospel: Mark 16:1–8

RESURRECTION OF THE LORD, EASTER DAY

First Reading: Acts 10:34–43 or Isaiah 25:6–9
Psalm 118:1–2, 14–24
Second Reading: 1 Corinthians 15:1–11 or Acts 10:34–43
Gospel: John 20:1–18 or Mark 16:1–8

EASTER EVENING (A,B,C)

The following readings are for occasions when the main (eucharistic) Easter service must be late in the day. They are not intended for Vespers (Evening Prayer) on Easter Evening.

Isaiah 25:6–9
Psalm 114
1 Corinthians 5:6b–8
Luke 24:13–49

SECOND SUNDAY OF EASTER

Acts 4:32–35
Psalm 133
1 John 1:1–2:2
John 20:19–31

THIRD SUNDAY OF EASTER

Acts 3:12–19
Psalm 4
1 John 3:1–7
Luke 24:36b–48

FOURTH SUNDAY OF EASTER

Acts 4:5–12
Psalm 23
1 John 3:16–24
John 10:11–18

FIFTH SUNDAY OF EASTER

Acts 8:26–40
Psalm 22:25–31
1 John 4:7–21
John 15:1–8

SIXTH SUNDAY OF EASTER

Acts 10:44–48
Psalm 98
1 John 5:1–6
John 15:9–17

ASCENSION OF THE LORD (A,B,C)

The following readings may also be used on Seventh Sunday of Easter.

Acts 1:1–11
Psalm 47 or Psalm 93
Ephesians 1:15–23
Luke 24:44–53

SEVENTH SUNDAY OF EASTER

Acts 1:15–17, 21–26
Psalm 1

1 John 5:9–13
John 17:6–19

DAY OF PENTECOST
If the passage from Ezekiel is chosen for the First Reading, the passage from Acts is used as the Second Reading.

First Reading: Acts 2:1–21 or Ezekiel 37:1–14
Psalm 104:24–34, 35b
Second Reading: Romans 8:22–27 or Acts 2:1–21
Gospel: John 15:26–27; 16:4b–15

Season After Pentecost (Ordinary Time)

TRINITY SUNDAY (FIRST SUNDAY AFTER PENTECOST)
Isaiah 6:1–8
Psalm 29
Romans 8:12–17
John 3:1–17

If the Sunday between May 24 and 28 inclusive follows Trinity Sunday, the Proper for the Eighth Sunday after the Epiphany [8] is used.

PROPER 4 [9]

SUNDAY BETWEEN MAY 29 AND JUNE 4 INCLUSIVE (If after Trinity Sunday)

1 Samuel 3:1–10, (11–20) with Psalm 139:1–6, 13–18 or
Deuteronomy 5:12–15 with Psalm 81:1–10
2 Corinthians 4:5–12
Mark 2:23–3:6

PROPER 5 [10]

SUNDAY BETWEEN JUNE 5 AND JUNE 11 INCLUSIVE (If after Trinity Sunday)

1 Samuel 8:4–11, (12–15), 16–20 with Psalm 130 or
Genesis 3:8–15 (11:14–15) with Psalm 138
2 Corinthians 4:13–5:1
Mark 3:20–35

Pʀᴏᴘᴇʀ 6 [11]

SUNDAY BETWEEN JUNE 12 AND JUNE 18 INCLUSIVE (If after Trinity Sunday)

1 Samuel 15:34–16:13 with Psalm 20 or
Ezekiel 17:22–24 with Psalm 92:1–4, 12–15
2 Corinthians 5:6–10, (11–13), 14–17
Mark 4:26–34

Pʀᴏᴘᴇʀ 7 [12]

SUNDAY BETWEEN JUNE 19 AND JUNE 25 INCLUSIVE (If after Trinity Sunday)

1 Samuel 17:32–49 (1a, 4–11, 19–23) with Psalm 9:9–20 or
1 Samuel 17:57–18:5, 10–16 with Psalm 133 or
Job 38:1–11 with Psalm 107:1–3, 23–32
2 Corinthians 6:1–13
Mark 4:35–41

Pʀᴏᴘᴇʀ 8 [13]

SUNDAY BETWEEN JUNE 26 AND JULY 2 INCLUSIVE

2 Samuel 1:1, 17–27 with Psalm 130 or
Wisdom of Solomon 1:13–15; 2:23–24 or
Lamentations 3:23–33 with Psalm 30
2 Corinthians 8:7–15
Mark 5:21–43

Pʀᴏᴘᴇʀ 9 [14]

SUNDAY BETWEEN JULY 3 AND JULY 9 INCLUSIVE

2 Samuel 5:1–5, 9–10 with Psalm 48 or
Ezekiel 2:1–5 with Psalm 123
2 Corinthians 12:2–10
Mark 6:1–13

Pʀᴏᴘᴇʀ 10 [15]

SUNDAY BETWEEN JULY 10 AND JULY 16 INCLUSIVE

2 Samuel 6:1–5, 12b–19 with Psalm 24 or
Amos 7:7–15 with Psalm 85:8–13

Ephesians 1:3–14
Mark 6:14–29

PROPER 11 [16]

SUNDAY BETWEEN JULY 17 AND JULY 23 INCLUSIVE

2 Samuel 7:1–14a with Psalm 89:20–37 or
Jeremiah 23:1–6 with Psalm 23
Ephesians 2:11–22
Mark 6:30–34, 53–56

PROPER 12 [17]

SUNDAY BETWEEN JULY 24 AND JULY 30 INCLUSIVE

2 Samuel 11:1–15 with Psalm 14 or
2 Kings 4:42–44 with Psalm 145:10–18
Ephesians 3:14–21
John 6:1–21

PROPER 13 [18]

SUNDAY BETWEEN JULY 31 AND AUGUST 6 INCLUSIVE

2 Samuel 11:26–12:13a with Psalm 51:1–12 or
Exodus 16:2–4, 9–15 with Psalm 78:23–29
Ephesians 4:1–16
John 6:24–35

PROPER 14 [19]

SUNDAY BETWEEN AUGUST 7 AND AUGUST 13 INCLUSIVE

2 Samuel 18:5–9, 15, 31–33 with Psalm 130 or
1 Kings 19:4–8 with Psalm 34:1–8
Ephesians 4:25–5:2
John 6:35, 41–51

PROPER 15 [20]

SUNDAY BETWEEN AUGUST 14 AND AUGUST 20

1 Kings 2:10–12; 3:3–14 with Psalm 111 or
Proverbs 9:1–6 with Psalm 34:9–14

Ephesians 5:15–20
John 6:51–58

PROPER 16 [21]

SUNDAY BETWEEN AUGUST 21 AND AUGUST 27
INCLUSIVE

1 Kings 8:(1, 6, 10–11), 22–30, 41–43 with Psalm 84 or
Joshua 24:1–2a, 14–18 with Psalm 34:15–22
Ephesians 6:10–20
John 6:56–69

PROPER 17 [22]

SUNDAY BETWEEN AUGUST 28 AND SEPTEMBER 3
INCLUSIVE

Song of Solomon 2:8–13 with Psalm 45:1–2, 6–9 or
Deuteronomy 4:1–2, 6–9 with Psalm 15
James 1:17–27
Mark 7:1–8, 14–15, 21–23

PROPER 18 [23]

SUNDAY BETWEEN SEPTEMBER 4 AND SEPTEMBER 10
INCLUSIVE

Proverbs 22:1–2, 8–9, 22–23 with Psalm 125 or
Isaiah 35:4–7a with Psalm 146
James 2:1–10, (11–13), 14–17
Mark 7:24–37

PROPER 19 [24]

SUNDAY BETWEEN SEPTEMBER 11 AND SEPTEMBER 17
INCLUSIVE

Proverbs 1:20–33 with Psalm 19 or
Isaiah 50:4–9a or Wisdom of Solomon 7:26–8:1 with
Psalm 116:1–9
James 3:1–12
Mark 8:27–38

PROPER 20 [25]

SUNDAY BETWEEN SEPTEMBER 18 AND SEPTEMBER 24 INCLUSIVE

Proverbs 31:10–31 with Psalm 1 or
Wisdom of Solomon 1:16–2:1, 12–22 or
Jeremiah 11:18–20 with Psalm 54
James 3:13–4:3, 7–8a
Mark 9:30–37

PROPER 21 [26]

SUNDAY BETWEEN SEPTEMBER 25 AND OCTOBER 1 INCLUSIVE

Esther 7:1–6, 9–10; 9:20–22 with Psalm 124 or
Numbers 11:4–6, 10–16, 24–29 with Psalm 19:7–14
James 5:13–20
Mark 9:38–50

PROPER 22 [27]

SUNDAY BETWEEN OCTOBER 2 AND OCTOBER 8 INCLUSIVE

Job 1:1; 2:1–10 with Psalm 26 or
Genesis 2:18–24 with Psalm 8
Hebrews 1:1–4; 2:5–12
Mark 10:2–16

PROPER 23 [28]

SUNDAY BETWEEN OCTOBER 9 AND OCTOBER 15 INCLUSIVE

Job 23:1–9, 16–17 with Psalm 22:1–15 or
Amos 5:6–7, 10–15 with Psalm 90:12–17
Hebrews 4:12–16
Mark 10:17–31

PROPER 24 [29]

SUNDAY BETWEEN OCTOBER 16 AND OCTOBER 22 INCLUSIVE

Job 38:1–7, (34–41) with Psalm 104:1–9, 24, 35c or
Isaiah 53:4–12 with Psalm 91:9–16

Hebrews 5:1–10
Mark 10:35–45

PROPER 25 [30]

SUNDAY BETWEEN OCTOBER 23 AND OCTOBER 29
INCLUSIVE

Job 42:1–6, 10–17 with Psalm 34:1–8, (19–22) or
Jeremiah 31:7–9 with Psalm 126
Hebrews 7:23–28
Mark 10:46–52

PROPER 26 [31]

SUNDAY BETWEEN OCTOBER 30 AND NOVEMBER 5
INCLUSIVE

Ruth 1:1–18 with Psalm 146 or
Deuteronomy 6:1–9 with Psalm 119:1–8
Hebrews 9:11–14
Mark 12:28–34

PROPER 27 [32]

SUNDAY BETWEEN NOVEMBER 6 AND NOVEMBER 12
INCLUSIVE

Ruth 3:1–5; 4:13–17 with Psalm 127 or
1 Kings 17:8–16 with Psalm 146
Hebrews 9:24–28
Mark 12:38–44

PROPER 28 [33]

SUNDAY BETWEEN NOVEMBER 13 AND NOVEMBER 19
INCLUSIVE

1 Samuel 1:4–20 with 1 Samuel 2:1–10 or
Daniel 12:1–3 with Psalm 16
Hebrews 10:11–14, (15–18), 19–25
Mark 13:1–8

PROPER 29 [34] (Reign of Christ or Christ the King)

SUNDAY BETWEEN NOVEMBER 20 AND NOVEMBER 26
INCLUSIVE

2 Samuel 23:1–7 with Psalm 132:1–12, (13–18) or
Daniel 7:9–10, 13–14 with Psalm 93
Revelation 1:4b–8
John 18:33–37

ALL SAINTS, NOVEMBER 1 OR THE FIRST SUNDAY IN
NOVEMBER

Wisdom of Solomon 3:1–9 or Isaiah 25:6–9
Psalm 24
Revelation 21:1–6a
John 11:32–44

THANKSGIVING DAY (Fourth Thursday in November in the
United States; Second Monday in October in Canada)

Joel 2:21–27
Psalm 126
1 Timothy 2:1–7
Matthew 6:25–33

YEAR C

Begins on the First Sunday of Advent in 1997, 2000, 2003, 2006, 2009.

Season of Advent

FIRST SUNDAY OF ADVENT

Jeremiah 33:14–16
Psalm 25:1–10
1 Thessalonians 3:9–13
Luke 21:25–36

SECOND SUNDAY OF ADVENT

Baruch 5:1–9 or Malachi 3:1–4
Luke 1:68–79
Philippians 1:3–11
Luke 3:1–6

THIRD SUNDAY OF ADVENT

Zephaniah 3:14–20
Isaiah 12:2–6
Philippians 4:4–7
Luke 3:7–18

FOURTH SUNDAY OF ADVENT

Micah 5:2–5a
Luke 1:47–55 or Psalm 80:1–7
Hebrews 10:5–10
Luke 1:39–45, (46–55)

Season of Christmas

Nativity of the Lord (Christmas Day)

Any of the following three Propers may be used on Christmas Eve/Day.

The readings from Propers II and III for Christmas may be used as alternatives for Christmas Day. If Proper III is not used on Christmas Day, it should be used at some service during the Christmas cycle because of the significance of John's prologue.

CHRISTMAS, PROPER I (A,B,C)

Isaiah 9:2–7
Psalm 96
Titus 2:11–14
Luke 2:1–14, (15–20)

CHRISTMAS, PROPER II (A,B,C)

Isaiah 62:6–12
Psalm 97
Titus 3:4–7
Luke 2:(1–7), 8–20

CHRISTMAS, PROPER III (A,B,C)

Isaiah 52:7–10
Psalm 98
Hebrews 1:1–4, (5–12)
John 1:1–14

FIRST SUNDAY AFTER CHRISTMAS DAY

The following readings are used on the First Sunday after Christmas unless the readings for the Epiphany of the Lord are preferred.

1 Samuel 2:18–20, 26
Psalm 148
Colossians 3:12–17
Luke 2:41–52

JANUARY 1—HOLY NAME OF JESUS (MARY, MOTHER OF GOD) (A,B,C)

Numbers 6:22–27
Psalm 8
Galatians 4:4–7 or Philippians 2:5–11
Luke 2:15–21

JANUARY 1—WHEN OBSERVED AS NEW YEAR (A,B,C)

Ecclesiastes 3:1–13
Psalm 8
Revelation 21:1–6a
Matthew 25:31–46

SECOND SUNDAY AFTER CHRISTMAS DAY (A,B,C)

The following readings are provided for use when Epiphany (January 6) is celebrated on a weekday following the Second Sunday after Christmas Day.

Jeremiah 31:7–14 or Sirach 24:1–12
Psalm 147:12–20 or Wisdom of Solomon 10:15–21
Ephesians 1:3–14
John 1:(1–9), 10–18

Season of Epiphany (Ordinary Time)

EPIPHANY OF THE LORD (A,B,C)

Isaiah 60:1–6
Psalm 72:1–7, 10–14
Ephesians 3:1–12
Matthew 2:1–12

BAPTISM OF THE LORD [1] (FIRST SUNDAY AFTER THE EPIPHANY)

Isaiah 43:1–7
Psalm 29
Acts 8:14–17
Luke 3:15–17, 21–22

SECOND SUNDAY AFTER THE EPIPHANY [2]

Isaiah 62:1–5
Psalm 36:5–10
1 Corinthians 12:1–11
John 2:1–11

THIRD SUNDAY AFTER THE EPIPHANY [3]

Nehemiah 8:1–3, 5–6, 8–10
Psalm 19

1 Corinthians 12:12–31a
Luke 4:14–21

FOURTH SUNDAY AFTER THE EPIPHANY [4]

Jeremiah 1:4–10
Psalm 71:1–6
1 Corinthians 13:1–13
Luke 4:21–30

FIFTH SUNDAY AFTER THE EPIPHANY [5]

Isaiah 6:1–8, (9–13)
Psalm 138
1 Corinthians 15:1–11
Luke 5:1–11

SIXTH SUNDAY AFTER THE EPIPHANY [6]

Proper 1. If this is the Sunday before Ash Wednesday, this **Proper** may be replaced, in those churches using Transfiguration readings on this day, by the readings for the Last Sunday after the Epiphany.

Jeremiah 17:5–10
Psalm 1
1 Corinthians 15:12–20
Luke 6:17–26

SEVENTH SUNDAY AFTER THE EPIPHANY [7]

Proper 2. If this is the Sunday before Ash Wednesday, this Proper may be replaced, in those churches using Transfiguration readings on this day, by the readings for the Last Sunday after the Epiphany.

Genesis 45:3–11, 15
Psalm 37:1–11, 39–40
1 Corinthians 15:35–38, 42–50
Luke 6:27–38

EIGHTH SUNDAY AFTER THE EPIPHANY [8]

Proper 3. If this is the Sunday before Ash Wednesday, this Proper may be replaced, in those churches using Transfiguration readings on this day, by the readings for the Last Sunday after the Epiphany.

Sirach 27:4–7 or Isaiah 55:10–13
Psalm 92:1–4, 12–15
1 Corinthians 15:51–58
Luke 6:39–49

NINTH SUNDAY AFTER THE EPIPHANY [9]

Proper 4. The following readings are for churches whose calendar requires this Sunday, and do not observe the Last Sunday after the Epiphany as Transfiguration.

1 Kings 8:22–23, 41–43
Psalm 96:1–9
Galatians 1:1–12
Luke 7:1–10

LAST SUNDAY AFTER THE EPIPHANY (TRANSFIGURATION SUNDAY)

The following readings are used in churches where the Last Sunday after the Epiphany is observed as Transfiguration Sunday.

Exodus 34:29–35
Psalm 99
2 Corinthians 3:12–4:2
Luke 9:28–36, (37–43)

Season of Lent

ASH WEDNESDAY (A,B,C)

Joel 2:1–2, 12–17 or Isaiah 58:1–12
Psalm 51:1–17
2 Corinthians 5:20b–6:10
Matthew 6:1–6, 16–21

FIRST SUNDAY IN LENT

Deuteronomy 26:1–11
Psalm 91:1–2, 9–16
Romans 10:8b–13
Luke 4:1–13

SECOND SUNDAY IN LENT

Genesis 15:1–12, 17–18
Psalm 27
Philippians 3:17–4:1
Luke 13:31–35 or Luke 9:28–36

THIRD SUNDAY IN LENT

Isaiah 55:1–9
Psalm 63:1–8
1 Corinthians 10:1–13
Luke 13:1–9

FOURTH SUNDAY IN LENT

Joshua 5:9–12
Psalm 32
2 Corinthians 5:16–21
Luke 15:1–3, 11b–32

FIFTH SUNDAY IN LENT

Isaiah 43:16–21
Psalm 126
Philippians 3:4b–14
John 12:1–8

SIXTH SUNDAY IN LENT (PASSION SUNDAY or PALM SUNDAY)

Those who do not observe the procession with palms and do not wish to use the passion Gospel may substitute the Gospel and Psalm given for the Liturgy of the Passion with the Gospel and Psalm indicated for the Liturgy of the Palms. Whenever possible, the whole passion narrative should be read.

Liturgy of the Palms:
Luke 19:28–40
Psalm 118:1–2, 19–29

Liturgy of the Passion:
Isaiah 50:4–9a
Psalm 31:9–16
Philippians 2:5–11
Luke 22:14–23:56 or Luke 23:1–49

Holy Week

MONDAY OF HOLY WEEK (A,B,C)

Isaiah 42:1–9
Psalm 36:5–11
Hebrews 9:11–15
John 12:1–11

TUESDAY OF HOLY WEEK (A,B,C)

Isaiah 49:1–7
Psalm 71:1–14
1 Corinthians 1:18–31
John 12:20–36

WEDNESDAY OF HOLY WEEK (A,B,C)

Isaiah 50:4–9a
Psalm 70
Hebrews 12:1–3
John 13:21–32

HOLY THURSDAY (A,B,C)

Exodus 12:1–4, (5–10), 11–14
Psalm 116:1–2, 12–19
1 Corinthians 11:23–26
John 13:1–17, 31b–35

GOOD FRIDAY (A,B,C)

Isaiah 52:13–53:12
Psalm 22
Hebrews 10:16–25 or Hebrews 4:14–16; 5:7–9
John 18:1–19:42

HOLY SATURDAY (A,B,C)

The following readings are for use at services other than the Easter Vigil.

Job 14:1–14 or Lamentations 3:1–9, 19–24
Psalm 31:1–4, 15–16
1 Peter 4:1–8
Matthew 27:57–66 or John 19:38–42

Season of Easter

RESURRECTION OF THE LORD, EASTER VIGIL (A,B,C)

The following readings and psalms are provided for use at the Easter Vigil. A minimum of three Old Testament readings should be chosen. The reading from Exodus 14 should always be used.

Old Testament Readings and Psalms (A,B,C):
Genesis 1:1–2:4a with Psalm 136:1–9, 23–26
Genesis 7:1–5, 11–18; 8:6–18; 9:8–13 with Psalm 46
Genesis 22:1–18 with Psalm 16
Exodus 14:10–31; 15:20–21 with Exodus 15:1b–13, 17–18
Isaiah 55:1–11 with Isaiah 12:2–6
Baruch 3:9–15, 32–4:4 or Proverbs 8:1–8, 19–21; 9:4b–6 with
    Psalm 19
Ezekiel 36:24–28 with Psalm 42 and 43
Ezekiel 37:1–14 with Psalm 143
Zephaniah 3:14–20 with Psalm 98

New Testament Reading (A,B,C):
Romans 6:3–11
Psalm 114
Gospel: Luke 24:1–12

RESURRECTION OF THE LORD, EASTER DAY

First Reading: Acts 10:34–43 or Isaiah 65:17–25
Psalm 118:1–2, 14–24
Second Reading: 1 Corinthians 15:19–26 or Acts 10:34–43
Gospel: John 20:1–18 or Luke 24:1–12

EASTER EVENING (A,B,C)

The following readings are for occasions when the main (eucharistic) Easter service must be late in the day. They are not intended for Vespers (Evening Prayer) on Easter Evening.

Isaiah 25:6–9
Psalm 114
1 Corinthians 5:6b–8
Luke 24:13–49

SECOND SUNDAY OF EASTER

Acts 5:27–32
Psalm 118:14–29 or Psalm 150
Revelation 1:4–8
John 20:19–31

THIRD SUNDAY OF EASTER

Acts 9:1–6, (7–20)
Psalm 30
Revelation 5:11–14
John 21:1–19

FOURTH SUNDAY OF EASTER

Acts 9:36–43
Psalm 23
Revelation 7:9–17
John 10:22–30

FIFTH SUNDAY OF EASTER

Acts 11:1–18
Psalm 148
Revelation 21:1–6
John 13:31–35

SIXTH SUNDAY OF EASTER

Acts 16:9–15
Psalm 67
Revelation 21:10, 22–22:5
John 14:23–29 or John 5:1–9

ASCENSION OF THE LORD (A,B,C)

The following readings may also be used on the Seventh Sunday of Easter.

Acts 1:1–11
Psalm 47 or Psalm 93
Ephesians 1:15–23
Luke 24:44–53

SEVENTH SUNDAY OF EASTER

Acts 16:16–34
Psalm 97

Revelation 22:12–14, 16–17, 20–21
John 17:20–26

DAY OF PENTECOST
If the passage from Genesis is chosen for the First Reading, the passage from Acts is used as the Second Reading.

First Reading: Acts 2:1–21 or Genesis 11:1–9
Psalm 104:24–34, 35b
Second Reading: Romans 8:14–17 or Acts 2:1–21
Gospel: John 14:8–17, (25–27)

Season After Pentecost (Ordinary Time)

TRINITY SUNDAY (FIRST SUNDAY AFTER PENTECOST)

Proverbs 8:1–4, 22–31
Psalm 8
Romans 5:1–5
John 16:12–15

If the Sunday between May 24 and 28 inclusive follows Trinity Sunday, the Proper for the Eighth Sunday after the Epiphany [8] is used.

PROPER 4 [9]

SUNDAY BETWEEN MAY 29 AND JUNE 4 INCLUSIVE (If after Trinity Sunday)

1 Kings 18:20–21, (22–29), 30–39 with Psalm 96 or
1 Kings 8:22–23, 41–43 with Psalm 96:1–9
Galatians 1:1–12
Luke 7:1–10

PROPER 5 [10]

SUNDAY BETWEEN JUNE 5 AND JUNE 11 INCLUSIVE (If after Trinity Sunday)

1 Kings 17:8–16, (17–24) with Psalm 146 or
1 Kings 17:17–24 with Psalm 30
Galatians 1:11–24
Luke 7:11–17

PROPER 6 [11]

SUNDAY BETWEEN JUNE 12 AND JUNE 18 INCLUSIVE (If after Trinity Sunday)

1 Kings 21:1–10, (11–14), 15–21a with Psalm 5:1–8 or
2 Samuel 11:26–12:10, 13–15 with Psalm 32
Galatians 2:15–21
Luke 7:36–8:3

PROPER 7 [12]

SUNDAY BETWEEN JUNE 19 AND JUNE 25 INCLUSIVE (If after Trinity Sunday)

1 Kings 19:1–4, (5–7), 8–15a with Psalm 42 and 43 or
Isaiah 65:1–9 with Psalm 22:19–28
Galatians 3:23–29
Luke 8:26–39

PROPER 8 [13]

SUNDAY BETWEEN JUNE 26 AND JULY 2 INCLUSIVE

2 Kings 2:1–2, 6–14 with Psalm 77:1–2, 11–20 or
1 Kings 19:15–16, 19–21 with Psalm 16
Galatians 5:1, 13–25
Luke 9:51–62

PROPER 9 [14]

SUNDAY BETWEEN JULY 3 AND JULY 9 INCLUSIVE

2 Kings 5:1–14 with Psalm 30 or
Isaiah 66:10–14 with Psalm 66:1–9
Galatians 6:(1–6), 7–16
Luke 10:1–11, 16–20

PROPER 10 [15]

SUNDAY BETWEEN JULY 10 AND JULY 16 INCLUSIVE

Amos 7:7–17 with Psalm 82 or
Deuteronomy 30:9–14 with Psalm 25:1–10
Colossians 1:1–14
Luke 10:25–37

PROPER 11 [16]

SUNDAY BETWEEN JULY 17 AND JULY 23 INCLUSIVE

Amos 8:1–12 with Psalm 52 or
Genesis 18:1–10a with Psalm 15
Colossians 1:15–28
Luke 10:38–42

PROPER 12 [17]

SUNDAY BETWEEN JULY 24 AND JULY 30 INCLUSIVE

Hosea 1:2–10 with Psalm 85 or
Genesis 18:20–32
Psalm 138
Colossians 2:6–15, (16–19)
Luke 11:1–13

PROPER 13 [18]

SUNDAY BETWEEN JULY 31 AND AUGUST 6 INCLUSIVE

Hosea 11:1–11 with Psalm 107:1–9, 43 or
Ecclesiastes 1:2, 12–14; 2:18–23 with Psalm 49:1–12
Colossians 3:1–11
Luke 12:13–21

PROPER 14 [19]

SUNDAY BETWEEN AUGUST 7 AND AUGUST 13 INCLUSIVE

Isaiah 1:1, 10–20 with Psalm 50:1–8, 22–23 or
Genesis 15:1–6 with Psalm 33:12–22
Hebrews 11:1–3, 8–16
Luke 12:32–40

PROPER 15 [20]

SUNDAY BETWEEN AUGUST 14 AND AUGUST 20
INCLUSIVE

Isaiah 5:1–7 with Psalm 80:1–2, 8–19 or
Jeremiah 23:23–29 with Psalm 82
Hebrews 11:29–12:2
Luke 12:49–56

PROPER 16 [21]

SUNDAY BETWEEN AUGUST 21 AND AUGUST 27
INCLUSIVE

Jeremiah 1:4–10 with Psalm 71:1–6 or
Isaiah 58:9b–14 with Psalm 103:1–8
Hebrews 12:18–29
Luke 13:10–17

PROPER 17 [22]

SUNDAY BETWEEN AUGUST 28 AND SEPTEMBER 3
INCLUSIVE

Jeremiah 2:4–13 with Psalm 81:1, 10–16 or
Sirach 10:12–18 or Proverbs 25:6–7 with Psalm 112
Hebrews 13:1–8, 15–16
Luke 14:1, 7–14

PROPER 18 [23]

SUNDAY BETWEEN SEPTEMBER 4 AND SEPTEMBER 10
INCLUSIVE

Jeremiah 18:1–11 with Psalm 139:1–6, 13–18 or
Deuteronomy 30:15–20 with Psalm 1
Philemon 1–21
Luke 14:25–33

PROPER 19 [24]

SUNDAY BETWEEN SEPTEMBER 11 AND SEPTEMBER 17
INCLUSIVE

Jeremiah 4:11–12, 22–28 with Psalm 14 or
Exodus 32:7–14 with Psalm 51:1–10
1 Timothy 1:12–17
Luke 15:1–10

PROPER 20 [25]

SUNDAY BETWEEN SEPTEMBER 18 AND SEPTEMBER 24
INCLUSIVE

Jeremiah 8:18–9:1 with Psalm 79:1–9 or
Amos 8:4–7 with Psalm 113

1 Timothy 2:1–7
Luke 16:1–13

PROPER 21 [26]

SUNDAY BETWEEN SEPTEMBER 25 AND OCTOBER 1
INCLUSIVE

Jeremiah 32:1–3a, 6–15 with Psalm 91:1–6, 14–16 or
Amos 6:1a, 4–7 with Psalm 146
1 Timothy 6:6–19
Luke 16:19–31

PROPER 22 [27]

SUNDAY BETWEEN OCTOBER 2 AND OCTOBER 8
INCLUSIVE

Lamentations 1:1–6; 3:19–26 with Psalm 137 or
Habakkuk 1:1–4; 2:1–4 with Psalm 37:1–9
2 Timothy 1:1–14
Luke 17:5–10

PROPER 23 [28]

SUNDAY BETWEEN OCTOBER 9 AND OCTOBER 15
INCLUSIVE

Jeremiah 29:1, 4–7 with Psalm 66:1–12 or
2 Kings 5:1–3, 7–15c with Psalm 111
2 Timothy 2:8–15
Luke 17:11–19

PROPER 24 [29]

SUNDAY BETWEEN OCTOBER 16 AND OCTOBER 22
INCLUSIVE

Jeremiah 31:27–34 with Psalm 119:97–104 or
Genesis 32:22–31 with Psalm 121
2 Timothy 3:14–4:5
Luke 18:1–8

PROPER 25 [30]

SUNDAY BETWEEN OCTOBER 23 AND OCTOBER 29
INCLUSIVE

Joel 2:23–32 with Psalm 65 or
Sirach 35:12–17 or Jeremiah 14:7–10, 19–22 with Psalm 84:1–7
2 Timothy 4:6–8, 16–18
Luke 18:9–14

PROPER 26 [31]

SUNDAY BETWEEN OCTOBER 30 AND NOVEMBER 5
INCLUSIVE

Habakkuk 1:1–4; 2:1–4 with Psalm 119:137–144 or
Isaiah 1:10–18 with Psalm 32:1–7
2 Thessalonians 1:1–4, 11–12
Luke 19:1–10

PROPER 27 [32]

SUNDAY BETWEEN NOVEMBER 6 AND NOVEMBER 12
INCLUSIVE

Haggai 1:15b–2:9 with Psalm 145:1–5, 17–21 or Psalm 98 or
Job 19:23–27a with Psalm 17:1–9
2 Thessalonians 2:1–5, 13–17
Luke 20:27–38

PROPER 28 [33]

SUNDAY BETWEEN NOVEMBER 13 AND NOVEMBER 19
INCLUSIVE

Isaiah 65:17–25 with Isaiah 12 or
Malachi 4:1–2a with Psalm 98
2 Thessalonians 3:6–13
Luke 21:5–19

PROPER 29 [34] (Reign of Christ or Christ the King)

SUNDAY BETWEEN NOVEMBER 20 AND NOVEMBER 26
INCLUSIVE

Jeremiah 23:1–6 with Luke 1:68–79 or
Jeremiah 23:1–6 with Psalm 46

Colossians 1:11–20
Luke 23:33–43

ALL SAINTS, NOVEMBER 1 OR THE FIRST SUNDAY IN NOVEMBER

Daniel 7:1–3, 15–18
Psalm 149
Ephesians 1:11–23
Luke 6:20–31

THANKSGIVING DAY (Fourth Thursday in November in the United States; Second Sunday in October in Canada)

Deuteronomy 26:1–11
Psalm 100
Philippians 4:4–9
John 6:25–35

Special Days (A,B,C)

FEBRUARY 2, PRESENTATION OF THE LORD (A,B,C)

Malachi 3:1–4
Psalm 84 or Psalm 24:7–10
Hebrews 2:14–18
Luke 2:22–40

MARCH 25, ANNUNCIATION OF THE LORD (A,B,C)

Isaiah 7:10–14
Psalm 45 or Psalm 40:5–10
Hebrews 10:4–10
Luke 1:26–38

MAY 31, VISITATION OF MARY TO ELIZABETH (A,B,C)

1 Samuel 2:1–10
Psalm 113
Romans 12:9–16b
Luke 1:39–57

SEPTEMBER 14, HOLY CROSS (A,B,C)

Numbers 21:4b–9
Psalm 98:1–5 or Psalm 78:1–2, 34–38
1 Corinthians 1:18–24
John 3:13–17

PEOPLE
IN THE BIBLE

Aaron

The elder brother of Moses, who served as his helper in freeing the Israelites from slavery in Egypt.

Abraham and Sarah

Abraham (also Abram) is considered the ancestor of Judaism, Christianity, and Islam. He and his wife, Sarah (also Sarai), were the parents of Isaac. God's promise of descendants to Abraham and Sarah is seen as the covenant in which the Hebrew people become God's chosen people.

Adam and Eve

Adam is a Hebrew word meaning "man" or "mankind." Adam and Eve are designated as the first man and woman in the creation stories in Genesis.

Ahab

A king of Israel married to Jezebel whose reign and interaction with Elijah is recorded in 1 Kings.

Alexander the Great

Son of Philip II of Macedon, taught by Aristotle, ruler of Greece known for his extensive conquests of the Persian empire, Middle Eastern region, and Egypt before his death at thirty-three years of age. His influence contributed to the Hellenization of many Jews and to the translation of the Hebrew Bible into Greek.

Amalak

Grandson of Esau (Genesis 36:12); also one of the clans in Edom (Genesis 36:16) who attacked the Israelites escaping from Egypt (Exodus 17:8–9) and continued to be engaged in conflicts with Israel until they were defeated in the reign of Hezekiah (1 Chronicles 4:43).

Ammon, Ammonites

Genesis 19:38 identifies Ben-'ammi, the grandson of Lot, as the father of the Ammonites, a Semitic people who lived on the edge of the Syrian Desert, where they engaged in conflicts with various Israelite tribes (Judges 10:9), were defeated by Saul's army (1 Samuel 11:8–11), and subsequently subdued by David's army under Joab's leadership (2 Samuel 11:1, 22–24; 12:26).

Amos

The first prophet whose writings were collected into a work about him rather than being incorporated into the story about the nation. Amos condemned injustice and announced impending doom if the people did not repent and change their ways.

Antiochus

A common name of several kings of the Seleucid dynasty of Syria. Antiochus III, father of Cleopatra, ruled Palestine and is probably the king referred to in Daniel 11:10–19. His youngest son, Antiochus IV, issued the edict that required all people to worship Zeus and outlawed Judaism—which led to the Maccabean rebellion.

Artaxerxes

King of Persia who authorized Ezra's trip to Jerusalem to rebuild the temple, then temporarily halted the reconstruction (Ezra 7:8, 11–26; 4:7–23). Nehemiah's completion of rebuilding the temple was also done under his reign.

Augustus

Title given by the Roman Senate to Gaius Julius Caesar Octavianus, who was emperor of the Roman Empire and ruled over the Mediterranean world at the time of the birth of Jesus Christ.

Balaam

A foreign prophet who was summoned by Balak, king of Moab, to curse Israel prior to their entry into Canaan. He instead spoke for the God of Israel in pronouncing blessings on Israel (Numbers 22:5–24:25).

Barnabas

A companion of Paul (Acts 11–19:22) who later separated from him over disagreements about including the Gentiles and about working with John Mark (Acts 15:36–39).

Bathsheba

Wife of Uriah, whom David killed when his adulterous relationship with Bathsheba resulted in pregnancy. This child died; Bathsheba later bore Solomon, who succeeded his father as king.

Caiaphas

The high priest in the trial of Jesus (Matthew 26:57).

Cain

Eldest son of Adam and Eve. When God accepted his brother Abel's offering but not his, Cain killed Abel, and when God confronted him, asked "Am I my brother's keeper?"

Christ

See Jesus Christ.

Cyrus

King of Persia who defeated Babylon and thus came to be perceived as the "Lord's anointed" (Isaiah 45:1) who would precede the restoration of Israel (Isaiah 44:28 and chapters 35, 40–55).

Daniel

Central figure in the Book of Daniel, his name meaning "God has judged." Daniel was a young Jewish man who remained loyal to his faith while serving in a foreign king's court. His most famous experience: surviving a night in a lions' den.

David

One of the great kings of Israel; he institutionalized the monarchy, solidified the nation's territory, and conceptualized and planned for the building of the temple.

Deborah

One of the judges who ruled Israel wisely; known for her military acumen.

Elijah

One of the primary prophets of the Hebrew Scriptures known for his miracles and his opposition to worship of the pagan god Baal and regarded as the forerunner of the coming day of the Lord (Malachi 4:5). John the Baptist and Jesus were both thought by some to be Elijah returned to life or to embody Elijah's spirit (Matthew 16:14). His ministry is recorded in 1 and 2 Kings.

Elisha

The disciple and successor of Elijah; a leader in prophetic circles in the northern kingdom who actively influenced the political life of the nation (2 Kings).

Esther

Jewish woman who became queen of Persia and was responsible for saving the Jews from death.

Esau

Eldest son of Jacob and Rebekah; twin brother of Jacob; traditional ancestor of Edomites (Genesis 25–27).

Eve

The first woman whom God created when he made man (the first creation story—Genesis 1:27) or when he formed her out of man's rib to be his helpmate (the second creation story—Genesis 2:18–25).

Ezekiel

Prophet during the time of the Babylonian Exile who spoke of the doom and destruction to come and after the fall of Jerusalem brought hope and a belief that God could bring life out of death.

Ezra

A priest who returned to Jerusalem after the Babylonian Exile and revived Judaism.

Gabriel

An angel or messenger from God who appears in Daniel, 1 and 2 Enoch (in the Apocrypha), and announces the birth of John the Baptist and Jesus in Luke.

Gamaliel

The first to hold the title "Rabban" ("our Master," "our Great One") rather than "Rabbi" ("my Master"); a respected Pharisaic member of the Sanhedrin, he taught Paul (Acts 22:3) and urged the Sanhedrin to refrain from killing Paul and the other disciples (Acts 5:34–39).

Gideon

Called by God to lead the Israelites in defeating the Midianites (Judges 6:11–8:35), he is known for unusual signs from God (dew on the ground but not the fleece).

Hagar

Egyptian maid of Sarah and mother of Abraham's first son; see Ishmael.

Hammurabi (also spelled Hammurapi)

King of Babylon during its "golden age"; known for the Code of Hammurabi (a law code).

Hannah

Mother of the prophet Samuel; after years of being unable to bear a child, she vowed that if she were granted a son, she would dedicate him to God.

Herod the Great

Son of Jewish converts, Herod was appointed governor of Galilee, then perhaps governor of Syria, and finally king of Judea, a post he held when Jesus was born.

Hezekiah

Son of Ahaz who succeeded him as king of Judah; known as a faithful and pious ruler (2 Kings 18:5) who supported religious reformation (2 Chronicles 29–31).

Isaac and Rebekah

Isaac, the son promised to Abraham and Sarah in their old age, married Rebekah; they were parents of Jacob (Israel) and Esau.

Isaiah

One of the major prophets of Israel whose prophetic ministry is recorded in the first part of the book of Isaiah and echoed in the latter sections and in 2 Kings 19–20.

Ishmael

The first son of Abraham born to Hagar, Sarah's Egyptian maid. He and his mother were banished from the family after Isaac was born. God provided water in the wilderness and Ishmael fathered twelve sons and a daughter (Genesis 16–25).

Jacob (Israel)

Younger twin son of Isaac and Rebekah, brother of Esau, husband of Leah and Rachel, and father of the twelve sons who were the ancestral basis of the twelve tribes of Israel.

James (brother of Jesus)

Probably the oldest of Jesus' brothers (listed first both in Matthew 13:55 and in Mark 6:3), who was a witness of the Resurrection (1 Corinthians 15:7) and a key leader of the church in Jerusalem.

Jeremiah

One of the major prophets of Israel from before the reforms of Josiah (621 BCE) to after the destruction of Jerusalem in 587 BCE. His message is reflected in the book named for him.

Jesus Christ

Jesus was the personal name of the Son of God whose title, Christ, is the basis of "Christian." The Hebrew form of Jesus was

Joshua, or Yehoshuah, meaning "Yahweh saves" or "Yahweh will save." The New Testament is the story of Jesus and the development of the Christian religion after his death and resurrection.

Job

The lead character in the book of Job, a man known for his faithfulness despite the horrendous calamities he experienced.

John (the apostle)

Son of Zebedee, brother of James, and one of the first disciples called by Jesus (Matthew 4:21–22); in the early church he was associated with Peter (Acts 1:13; 8:14–25) and respected as a "pillar of the community" (Galatians 2:9).

John the Baptist

A prophet, son of the priest Zechariah and Elizabeth, a relative of Mary, mother of Jesus. John called people to repent and be baptized and pointed to "the one who is coming," namely Jesus Christ. He baptized Jesus, inaugurating his ministry (Matthew 3; Mark 1; Luke 1, 3; John 1).

Jonah

The prophet sent to Nineveh who was swallowed by a whale when he refused to go on his mission; central character of the Book of Jonah.

Jonathan

Eldest son of Saul, known for his devoted friendship with David, who later provided for Jonathan's lame son, Mephibosheth.

Joseph

There were actually several Josephs in the Bible. In Genesis, Joseph was the son of Jacob and Rachel who was sold by his brothers to Egyptians. He became a leader in Egypt, ultimately providing food for his family, who migrated there during a famine. In the New Testament, Joseph was the husband of Mary, mother of Jesus.

Joshua

Commissioned as Moses' successor, he was one of the spies who surveyed Canaan (Numbers 13:8) and became the Israelite general who led the conquest of Canaan as recorded in the book of Joshua.

Josiah

Becoming king of Judah at the age of eight, Josiah was known as one of Judah's greatest kings both for his discovery of the "Book of the Law" in the temple and his religious reforms.

Judas Iscariot

One of the twelve apostles who served as treasurer for the group and ultimately betrayed Jesus.

Judas Maccabeus

Son of the priest Mattathias and leader of the Jewish revolt against King Antiochus IV Epiphanes; Judas captured Jerusalem and rededicated the temple.

Lazarus of Bethany

Brother of Mary and Martha, a friend of Jesus whom Jesus raises from the dead (John 11:1–44).

Luke

Follower of Jesus, companion of Paul, and author of the Gospel that bears his name and its companion volume, the Book of Acts.

Mark, John

Son of Mary of Jerusalem (Acts 12:12), he traveled with his cousin Barnabas and Paul (Acts 12–15). Some feel he wrote the Gospel of Mark; others, that he was the young man who fled away naked in the Garden of Gethsemane (Mark 14:51–52).

Mary, Mother of Jesus

Young, devout Jewess who gave birth to Jesus. The Magnificat, a song of praise, is ascribed to her (Luke 1:46–55).

Mary of Magdala, or Mary Magdalene

One of the Galilean women who followed Jesus. Jesus freed her from seven demons (Luke 8:2; Mark 16:9).

Mary and Martha

Sisters who, with their brother Lazarus, were close friends of Jesus' (Luke 10:38–42; John 11:1–12:8). Mary was identified as the contemplative learner, Martha as the worker.

Matthew

A tax collector who became one of the twelve apostles of Jesus (Matthew 10:3); in Mark 2:14 and Luke 5:27, 29, he is called Levi.

Melchizedek

Probably a Canaanite king in Jerusalem who prepared a cultic meal for Abram (Abraham), blessed him and received his tithe, and was identified as the representative king in whose line David was ordained (Psalm 110). In Hebrews (5:5–10; 6:20), Christ is named as "high priest after the order of Melchizedek."

Miriam

Sister of Moses and Aaron remembered for her song of victory at the drowning of the Egyptians in the Red Sea (Exodus 15:20–21), one of the earliest fragments of Hebrew poetry.

Moses

Led the Hebrew tribes out of captivity in Egypt (the Exodus) which became the defining event for the Israelite people. Moses received the Law and was the leader throughout the wilderness period before the Israelites entered the Promised Land.

Naomi

Elimelech's wife, who, upon the death of her husband and sons, returned to her native Bethlehem; her daughter-in-law, Ruth, returned with her, married Boaz (Elimelech's next of kin), and bore a son, Obed, who was David's grandfather.

Nebuchadnezzar

King of Babylon who captured Jerusalem and ended the kingdom of Judah as an independent political entity.

Nero

Roman emperor from 54–68 CE and persecutor of the early Christians; known for "fiddling while Rome burned," enjoying the good life and killing anyone who got in his way.

Nicodemus

A Jewish leader and teacher who secretly questioned Jesus about being "born again" and later supported him (John 7:50–52); helped prepare Jesus' body for burial (John 19:39).

Nehemiah

A prophet who, with Ezra, led the return of the exiles to Jerusalem and the rebuilding of the city and temple.

Noah

An early patriarch in the Hebrew Bible; he and his family survived the Flood (Genesis 9:20–29) due to his faithfulness and obedience.

Paul

An educated Hellenistic Jew named Saul who persecuted Christians until he had a vision of Christ and was transformed into the primary missionary to the Gentiles (and renamed Paul; see "Name" in Glossary of Terms).

Peter

A prominent apostle of Jesus also known as Cephas, Symeon, or Simon. He was the first to identify Jesus as the Messiah. Jesus named him Peter, the Rock. The Roman Catholic Church has seen Matthew 16:17–19 as establishing him as the father of the church.

Pilate, Pontius

The Roman procurator of Judea in 26–36 CE; the judge in the trial of Jesus.

Rachel

Younger daughter of Laban, who gave her as wife to Jacob only after he first gave him her older sister, Leah. Rachel was the mother of Joseph and Benjamin, two of the twelve ancestors of the tribes of Israel.

Rahab

The woman who saved the lives of the spies Joshua sent to Jericho by hiding them on her roof, telling the searchers they had left and then lowering them over the city walls on a rope. In return, she and her family were spared when the city was burned (Joshua 2:1–21; 6:17, 22–25).

Rameses II

Ruler of Egypt who enslaved many of the peoples who ultimately became the Hebrew nation. His long reign was known for his building projects and forty years of peace and prosperity; he was regarded as a god by many Egyptians.

Rebekah

Wife of Isaac and mother of Esau and Jacob; known for her beauty, hospitality, and, after twenty years of barrenness, birthing the twin boys in response to Isaac's prayer (Genesis 24 and 25).

Ruth

A Moabite woman married to a Hebrew who returned to Bethlehem with her mother-in-law, married her husband's kinsman, and gave birth to Obed, father of Jesse, father of King David. This made her an ancestor of Jesus'.

Samson

Born to a long-barren woman and dedicated as a Nazirite, he was known both for his conquest of the Philistines and for his superhuman strength, which he lost when Delilah cut his previously untouched hair (Judges 13–16).

Samuel

A prophet who anointed Saul and David as kings over Israel.

Sarah

Wife of Abraham, mother of Isaac; her name was changed from Sarai (Genesis 17:13).

Saul

The first king of Israel who served in the transition time between the loosely organized Hebrew tribes and the United Monarchy under David.

Simon Maccabeus

One of Mattathias's five sons, he became a respected leader of the rebellion against Syria and was ultimately the first high priest of Judea to be elected, rather than succeeding, to the office by birthright.

Solomon

David and Bathsheba's second son, who became the third king of Israel. He is known for his wisdom, his many wives, the building of the temple, and his oppressive rulership that resulted in dividing the kingdom when his son refused to ease the people's tax burdens.

Stephen

One of the seven men selected to help the apostles by serving tables and caring for the widows. He serves as a model for today's deacons in churches that have bishops, priests, and deacons as ordained ministers.

Zacchaeus

A tax collector in Jericho who climbed a tree to see Jesus and invited him to his house. Zacchaeus promised to make fourfold restitution to anyone he defrauded (Luke 19:1–10).

Zechariah

There are more than thirty Zechariahs in the Bible; key among these are a king of Israel (2 Kings 14:29; 15:8, 11), one of the twelve minor prophets (see the Book of Zechariah), and John the Baptist's father, struck mute as a sign that he would be given a son (Luke 1:5–67; 3:2).

Zedekiah

The last king of Judah, killed by the Babylonian king Nebuchadnezzar after the capture of Jerusalem.

PLACES IN THE BIBLE

Babylon

Capital city of Babylonia, where the Israelites were exported to live in captivity. Best-known kings in Babylonia were Hammurabi (1792–1750 BCE) and Nebuchadnezzar (605–562 BCE). Babylonia and Assyria were two civilizations in Mesopotamia (modern Iraq) between 2500 and about 300 BCE that fought for domination in the region. In Assyria the best-known rulers were Tiglath-Pileser I (1115–1076 BCE), Tiglath-Pileser II (966–935 BCE, the time of Solomon), and Tiglath-Pileser III (745–727 BCE).[3]

Bethel

A Canaanite sanctuary city dedicated to the god El, which was regarded as a holy site by the Hebrew people. Abraham built an altar there (Genesis 12:8) and God was named the God of Bethel in Genesis 13:13. Jacob had a vision, received a blessing from God, and pledged a tithe at this site (Genesis 28:10–22). The Ark of the Covenant was located there (Judges 20:18–28) and it was the site of the prophet Amos' ministry.

Bethlehem

Judean city where Jesus was born (Matthew 2:1; Luke 2:4–6).

Cana of Galilee

The village where Jesus turned water into wine at a wedding feast—his first recorded miracle after his baptism (John 2:1–11).

---

[3]"Assyria and Babylonia," *The Interpreter's Dictionary of the Bible* Volume A–D (New York: Abingdon Press, 1962), p. 268–274.

Canaan

The region west of the Jordan River which was called the Promised Land by the Hebrew people. This was the land God promised to Abraham (Genesis 12:4–9) and Moses as the place where the Hebrews were to go after being freed from slavery in Egypt (Genesis 23:28–31).

Capernaum

The city on the northwest shore of the Sea of Galilee where Jesus began his ministry after being tempted in the wilderness; it was his "home" and served as the center for much of his ministry.

Egypt

A powerful, wealthy nation in northern Africa, geographically defined by the Nile River. Jacob's family migrated there during a famine and later were enslaved and freed in the Exodus, a formative event in Israelite history.

Gabbatha

The place where Jesus is tried before Pilate; it is the paved court in front of the palace where the ruler held court (John 19:13).

Galilee

A region north and west of the Sea of Galilee which was the primary region where Jesus lived and traveled during his active ministry.

Gethsemane

The place where Jesus prayed on the Passover night before Judas betrayed him by bringing the authorities there to arrest him. Traditionally called "the Garden," it was a field, perhaps an olive grove on the Mount of Olives outside Jerusalem.

Israel

The name given to the Promised Land (Canaan) after the Israelites inhabited it. Also the name given to the northern kingdom when the United Kingdom was divided after the rule of King Solomon. The name comes from Jacob, son of Isaac and grandson of Abraham, who was renamed Israel after he wrestled with an angel (Genesis 32:22–28).

Jericho

The first city of Canaan to fall as Joshua led the Israelites into the Promised Land. Trumpets, shouts, and walks around the city culminated in its collapse (Joshua 6).

Jerusalem

The Holy City, Mount Zion, the city established by King David as the locus of religious and political life, the home of the temple, and the place where Jesus Christ was crucified. It is the sacred city for Jews and Christians and the third most holy city for Muslims. Jerusalem, in both the Hebrew and Christian Scriptures, is the "city of God," where at the end of time God's people will live in peace and harmony with God and one another.

Jordan River

The river in Palestine that cuts through the center of that part the Middle East where many of the biblical stories were set. The Hebrew people crossed the Jordan into the Promised Land and Jesus was baptized in this river.

Judah

The tribe of Hebrew peoples, descended from Judah, the fourth son of Jacob and Leah, that joined with other tribes in the southern half of what was the United Kingdom under David. When the kingdoms divided, Judah became a separate nation, later called Judea. Judea, Samaria, and Galilee comprise the area later called Palestine.

Nazareth

A small village roughly between the Mediterranean Sea and the Sea of Galilee which was the childhood home of Jesus.

Mount Gerizim

In early history it was a religious site visited by Abraham (Genesis 12:6), Jacob (Genesis 33:18–20), and Joshua (Joshua 8:33). Later, Samaritans saw it as a holy place and built temples there. To this day, some Samaritans celebrate Passover on its summit.

Mount of Olives

The mountain overlooking Jerusalem which served as the site for several events in the last week of Jesus' life and is mentioned as the last meeting of the disciples with the risen Christ before the Ascension.

Mount Sinai

The place where Moses received the law (Exodus 19–24) and God revealed God's presence to Moses and the people.

Nineveh

Capital of Assyria until its collapse in 612 BCE; one of the oldest cities in Mesopotamia. The prophet Jonah was sent to this city to warn of God's pending punishment.

Palestine

In ancient history it referred to the regions in the Near East dominated by Semitic languages. In the Hebrew Bible, "Philistia," primarily the seacoast plain, was usually referred to as Canaan or the Promised Land. This region was the focus of innumerable struggles between the Philistines, Canaanites, Hebrew tribes, and a host of other regional tribes and peoples who occupied portions of the land and often intermarried. The dispute over boundaries and peoples continues today.

Rome

Capital of the Roman Empire, which controlled the Mediterranean region during the time Christianity developed; today it is the capital of Italy.

Samaria

Capital of the southern kingdom of Israel until the city fell in 721 BCE, the name also refers to a region. Samaritans were the inhabitants of this region. There was and is a religious community living in that area. Samaritans claim to be the remnant of the southern kingdom of Israel; they have doctrines and an ancient version of the Pentateuch that differs from that accepted by Judaism. They also see Mount Gerizim rather than Jerusalem as God's holy place. Judaism views them as a largely heathen religion with some Jewish additions. Living under Muslim domination for many years led to their adopting Islamic practices.

Shechem

Ancient Canaanite city; important in Israelite religious and political life. Visited by Abraham and Jacob, burial place of Joseph and site of Joshua's assemblies of the tribes after the initial conquest of Canaan (Joshua 24:1).

Shiloh

City between Jerusalem and Shechem where the Ark of the Covenant and the tabernacles resided from Joshua (Joshua 18:1, 31) until the days of Samuel.

Sinai

See Mount Sinai.

GLOSSARY OF TERMS

Altar

A place of sacrifice. In the Hebrew Bible it was made of earth (Exodus 20:24), stone (Exodus 20:25), or bronze (2 Kings 16:15) and was the place of animal sacrifice. There was also an altar of incense (Exodus 30:27). The table for the bread of the Presence (1 Kings 6:20, 7:48) is a presentation altar (a place where offerings are presented to God). Christian altars originally were tables, later they were more like wooden boxes on which the bread and wine, the body and blood of Christ, were placed during the Eucharistic Prayer. In all cases the altar is a focal point for God's presence.

Angel

A messenger, usually a nonhuman celestial being. In the Bible angels sometimes function as intermediaries between God and people. Sometimes they are seen as God in a human form (e.g. the angels visiting Abraham in Genesis 18).

Anoint

To pour oil or ointment on someone or something. Done to promote healing of an injury or on a festive occasion, as in using perfumed ointments or anointing a guest. In religious ceremonies, anointing consecrated (i.e. set apart, made holy) the person or object. Priests and kings were anointed in this fashion.

Apostle

A messenger sent to act on behalf of the sender. Jesus named twelve of his disciples apostles: Andrew, Simon Peter, James,

John, Philip, Bartholomew, Matthew, Thomas, James (son of Alphaeus), Simon the Zealot, Judas (son of James), and Judas Iscariot (see Luke 6:12–16; 9:1–6).

Ark of the Covenant

A container that held the stone tablets on which the Ten Commandments were written (see Deuteronomy 10:1–5, where it is called the Ark of the Testimony). Later it became a focus for God's presence and was used in military and liturgical contexts (1 Samuel 4–7; Joshua 3:2–7). The P tradition calls it the Ark of Testimony.

Ascension

After Jesus was raised from the dead, he ascended. Since people believed God was "up" in heaven, he went "up." This type of poetic imagery, often used in Scripture and liturgy, is as close as we can come to defining this and other mysteries. The Ascension describes the mystery the disciples experienced—Jesus entering into a relationship with God where he shared God's rule over heaven and earth (Luke 24:51; Acts 1:9–11; Acts 5:31–32).

Atone, atonement

In the Hebrew Bible: taking away sins by doing something that turns away God's wrath or by "covering" the sin so it is not seen by God. The Day of Atonement was an annual feast in Judaism (Leviticus 16) when the priest atoned for the sins of the people. Today it is an occasion of confession, contrition (sorrow for wrongdoing), and thanksgiving for God's forgiveness in Judaism. In the New Testament Jesus' death and resurrection makes him "at one" with God. Our brokenness (sin) is healed and we come into full relationship with God through Christ when we confess our sin and ask for forgiveness. Christ's "at-one-ment" with God "covers" our sin, making it nonexistent and causing God to relate to us as if we had not committed the sin.

Baal

The storm god and fertility god of Canaan; sometimes refers to local manifestations of the deity, as in Baal-peor (the god of Mount Peor).

Baptize

To dip or plunge underwater; sometimes to wash. In the Christian Scripture, John plunges people underwater to show their repentance (turning away from sin) and to cleanse them from the effect of their sin (Mark 1:4ff). Christians are baptized for this reason and to unite them with Christ's death and resurrection, giving them a new life of being "at one" with God through Christ. Baptism is the way people become part of the Christian community (John 3:5; Romans 6:4).

Beatitudes

A literary form that begins with the word "blessed" and praises an individual whose behavior merits reward from God. In the Hebrew Bible, beatitudes are found primarily in the Psalms (e.g. 41:1; 84:5; 112:1). In the New Testament the term is used for the sayings in the Sermon on the Mount (Matthew 5:3–12; Luke 6:20–23).

Bitter herbs

Herbs eaten at Passover to symbolize the bitterness of the Hebrews' experience of slavery in Egypt.

Bless

The active giving of God's goodwill or grace that results in happiness and well-being. People ask for God's blessing; when they "bless" someone it is understood that they are announcing God's blessing on that person. People "bless" God by giving thanks for and praising God ("Blessed be the God . . ." 2 Corinthians 1:3). The opposite of "bless" is "curse."

Booths, Feast of

One of Israel's three annual festivals celebrated in the fall, after harvest. It remembered the years of wandering in the wilderness and later included a renewal of the covenant. It is also called the Feast of Tabernacles, Feast of Ingathering, and Feast of the Lord at Shiloh. It included the Day of Atonement (see Atonement). It is probably a conflation of several religious ceremonies and practices taken from both Israelite and Canaanite worship.

Bread of the Presence

An offering of bread was placed on a table in the Holy of Holies at all times (Exodus 25:30; Leviticus 24:5–9). It may have originally been offered as a meal for the deity but later was seen as a thank offering that was consumed by the priests.

Christ

"The Anointed One" from the Greek word *christos,* or "anointed" (see Anoint and Messiah). The name was often used for Jesus after his death and resurrection to show that Jesus has become the Christ, the Anointed One, in full relationship with God.

Christian

Those who are followers of Christ; used only in Acts 11:26; 26:28; and 1 Peter 4:16.

Chosen People, election

Election is a religious conviction that God has chosen an individual (e.g. Abraham), a group (the Jews), or place (Jerusalem) to be in a unique and exclusive relationship with God. It often gives special authority and requires special obligations (e.g. to obey the Law). In the Hebrew Bible, Jerusalem and the ancestral leaders, kings, and priests are chosen. In the New Testament, Jesus is God's Chosen One and chooses the twelve to be apostles.

Church

In Christian Scriptures the Greek term *ekklesia* (church) is first used for Christians gathered by the Apostles in Jerusalem who had received the Holy Spirit (Acts 5:11; 8:1–3). Later it meant the local Christian community (Acts 11:26), groups of Christians gathered in homes, or the "whole church" (all Christians: Acts 9:31). Paul's epistles are letters to these house churches. Only in the fourth century did Christians have special buildings set aside for meetings—what we now call churches.

Clean and unclean

If an object, person, or place is contaminated by a ritual, physical, or moral impurity, it becomes "unclean." The Hebrew Bible describes how one prevents this state of uncleanness or how one regains cleanness through rites of purification. Cleanness is associated with holiness; the people of Israel are God's holy people, so they are to keep themselves clean—free from contamination by immoral behavior, ritual impurity, or contact with physical things that are unclean (e.g. dead bodies, leprosy, menstrual blood).

Command, commandments, Law

The command of God is the underlying principle of everything: the action of God on us, shaping us to be who God created us to be. All commandments, laws, and rules are not to be followed unthinkingly (Matthew 23:23; 25:31ff.; Galatians 5:13–14), but they should help us understand the reality of God's world and how God shapes us. Ignoring them often results in breaking the covenant relationship God set up with us. The Ten Commandments (Exodus 20:1–17) spell out the basics of God's covenant with the Hebrew people. The Great Commandment (Matthew 22:34–40), which says love God with all that we are and each other as ourselves, was Jesus' primary principle or command.

Confess

Usually means to openly admit that someone (or the community) has acted in a way that breaks relationship with God and/or one another (Psalms 32:5). In the Christian Scripture to confess also means to acknowledge and declare that something is what it is ("every tongue should confess that Jesus Christ is Lord" [Philemon 2:11]).

Consecrate, consecration

To set apart or dedicate a person or thing for some sacred purpose, often for use in worship of God. Consecration implies giving the person or object a quality of holiness. Sanctified is a related word, especially in the New Testament; Christians are saints, that is, they are sanctified, made holy (1 Corinthians 1:2).

Covenant

A contract relationship between two parties. Conditional covenants contain both costs (obligations) and promises; unconditional covenants are promises given with no obligations. In Hebrew Scripture, God's covenant with the Hebrews promises that they will be God's people, protected and blessed by God if they keep God's commandments (live as God created them to live). In Christian Scripture, Jesus announces a new covenant (1 Corinthians 11:25) promising forgiveness of sins and a full relationship with God created through God's gift of Jesus and his life, death, and resurrection. In return, we are to love God and all people.

Cross

A stake or tree or other vertical object to which someone was bound. It provided a way of killing people that was very painful and shameful (it took a long time in a public place with the person often stripped naked). Jesus was nailed to the horizontal crossbars fastened to an upright stake; he died about six hours later (Matthew 27:27ff.; Mark 15:20–39).

Curtain of the temple

The curtain that separated the Holy of Holies from the rest of the temple. This curtain was ripped in two at the moment Jesus died (Matthew 27:51; Mark 15:38; Luke 23:45).

Deacon

One of the three "orders" of ministry in the church (deacon, priest, and bishop) mentioned and foreshadowed in the New Testament. The position focuses especially on the aspect of service (Acts 6:1–6).

Decalogue

The Ten Commandments.

Disciple

A learner, scholar, pupil, apprentice. In Christian Scripture it refers to those who learned from a teacher such as John (John 1:35) and, more frequently, to those men and women who traveled with, gathered around, and learned from Jesus.

Evil

In the Hebrew Bible, evil is something bad, harmful, something that causes pain, suffering, or unhappiness. Evil actions are those that harm someone (as judged by the injured person) or that break the covenant (the relationship) between God and people. By the time of Jesus, people believed in spirits that harmed people or "the evil one" (sometimes called "the devil"). Today many people believe there is a "harmful force" in the world created by the accumulated harmful actions of people over the centuries. This evil affects us as individuals and as communities.

Exile

The time when the Jews were transplanted from Judah (including Jerusalem) to Babylonia (from 587 BCE to 538, when they began to return).

Faith, the faith

A Hebrew concept meaning firmness, reliability, or steadfastness; in the Hebrew Scriptures a person with faith is made firm and steadfast (faithfulness). "Having faith in God" means relying on God, accepting what God offers as promises, and accepting the responsibilities that come with being in relationship with God. Faith is more than belief in a concept. In the Christian Scripture it is the conviction and trust that comes out of a personal relationship with God in Christ.

Flood, the

The Flood (Genesis 6–9) is the story of water covering the earth, killing every living thing except Noah, his family, and two of every creature taken into the ark Noah built at God's command. A version of this story is found in most ancient religions. In the Hebrew Bible, God sent the Flood as punishment for human corruption and a way to "start over." Its importance is in the Noahic covenant: God's blessing of Noah and promise never to destroy all things by a flood again.

Forgive

To "cover," "lift up," "carry away." In theological terms it refers to the removal of sin so it no longer stands as a barrier to a full relationship with God or another person. In the Bible forgiveness is an act of God, who graciously restores people to relationship. Forgiving other people becomes prominent in Jesus' teachings, where forgiveness is conditional on repentance: a deliberate change of mind and direction with an intention to live differently. This change in the sinner and the "release" or "removal" of the barrier by God and/or the injured person restores the relationship to wholeness. We need to forgive others in order to repent and be forgiven ourselves (Matthew 6:12; Mark 11:25ff.).

Gospel

The word comes from the Anglo-Saxon "godspell" or "God-story," used to translate the Greek *euangelion,* which means "good news." The good news preached by and about Jesus was that the full reign of God was at hand (Mark 1:15; Matt 10:7ff.; Luke 10:9). After the death and resurrection of Jesus, the good news is Christ himself as God incarnate (Mark 1:1,14; Romans 1:1). This good news is that God loved us so much that he gave his son Jesus, so anyone who believes in him will be in full relationship with God forever (John 3:16). Christians believe that this gospel must be received personally by faith.

Grace

A significant word used very differently in the Hebrew Scriptures and Christian Scriptures. In the Hebrew Bible grace (*chen*) means kindness and graciousness between two strangers or acquaintances or between a superior and inferior where the superior has no obligation to be kind. In the New Testament grace (*charis*) refers to God's love, which constantly acts to restore sinners to full relationship with God. This is more like the Hebrew term "loving-kindness" (*chesed*), which refers to God's determination to continue loving the Hebrew people, no matter what. That love is given freely by God and is unearned and undeserved. It is God's love that heals all the brokenness created by people and their actions. That love is most clearly seen in the life and sacrifice of Jesus Christ, Christians believe.

Hanukkah

Modern Jewish festival commemorating the reconsecration of the temple and altar by Judas Maccabeus in 165 BCE (1 Maccabees 4:52–59) in which a tiny bit of oil was found but miraculously burned for eight days. In the Hebrew Bible it is known as the Feast of Dedication, referring to various dedicatory celebrations. It is also known as the Feast of Lights after the ceremonial lighting of candles on each successive day of the eight-day feast.

Healing, health, wholeness

Restoring a sick person to health and wholeness; usually implies physical, mental, and spiritual health. In Hebrew *shalem* (healthy or whole) is a cognate of *shalom* (peace). The Hebrew Bible sees illness as sent by God as punishment. Many of the dietary and purification laws of Judaism are designed to maintain health; religious rites were designed to restore health by restoring the person to right relationship with God. Jesus did not see illness as divine punishment, but in some cases he attributed illness to the presence of evil in human life (Luke 13:16).

He understood the relationship between body, mind, and soul and made healing a central part of his ministry.

Holy Spirit

In the Hebrew Scriptures "spirit" refers to wind, breath, soul, and good or evil spirits (supernatural beings). God's Spirit had power to create and sustain life; it could enter people and impart wisdom, insight, and power. In the Christian Scriptures God's Spirit is present in and through Jesus and is given to those who believe in him (Acts 2:1; 20:16). The supernatural power of the Holy Spirit is seen in "gifts of the Spirit" such as healing, preaching, teaching, leading, prophesying.

Justice

This word rarely occurs in Scripture; the early Latin translations of the Bible used it to translate the Hebrew word which is best translated "righteousness." Righteousness means right action and fair dealings in one's relationship with God and every human being. What is just or right is determined by the nature of the relationship.

Kingdom of God, reign of God

A central theme of Jesus' teachings; refers to the time when God will act to break the power of evil and fully rule over people and the world God created. Jesus' life, death, and resurrection inaugurated that time by beginning to bring people and the world into what they were created to be. We glimpse this new condition in the miracles and teaching of Jesus, but the reign of God that Jesus started has not been consummated. It is an action by God that we participate in by accepting Jesus and living as he did: rejecting evil, receiving God's love, teaching the good news to others, and exercising God's power in the world.

Law

See Torah.

Liturgy

See Worship.

Love

One English word used to translate many different words. In the Hebrew Scripture it usually refers to *ahed,* meaning friendship, family affection, or passionate love between a man and a woman. Classical Greek has several words for love: *eros* (sexual or physical love; not used in the Christian Scriptures), *phileo/philia* (affection of friends), *philadelphia* (love between sisters, brothers), *stergo/storge* (family affection), *philanthropia* (human kindness, courtesy), and *agapazo, agapao* (to be content with, showing love by unselfish action). The New Testament uses *agape* to convey divine love that is personal, freely given, undeserved, unearned, and that shows itself by helping someone rather than wanting to possess someone. Christians are called to live out this divine love.

Messiah

The word means the "anointed one" in Hebrew. It originally referred to kings who were anointed with oil. It came to mean the one who would deliver Israel and Judah from their conquerors. Some Jews continue to wait for the Messiah whom God will raise up to restore the Kingdom of David (God's righteous rule). Christians see Jesus as the Messiah who has inaugurated God's righteous rule and will return to fulfill (complete) it. The word for Messiah—anointed one—in Greek is *Christos*.

Ministry

In Hebrew Scripture: the service of priests in the temple. In Christian Scripture: service of all (ordained and laity) on behalf of and in the name of Jesus Christ. It also is used for ministerial functions in the church: teaching, preaching, healing, and so on.

Miracle

Acts of power, mighty works, signs, and wonders; any natural or supernatural event in which someone sees God acting or sees God's self-revelation. In Hebrew Scripture the primary miracles are those associated with the Exodus or with Elijah and Elisha. In Christian Scripture the supreme miracle is the resurrection of Jesus, who also did acts of healing, raising people from the dead, stilling storms, and the like. This was to reveal who Jesus was and show the power of God. The Book of Acts indicates that some of Jesus' early followers also carried on his tradition of miracle working.

Myth

A story or explanation that expresses truth, interprets that which is real in symbolic and ideal terms, and/or puts a specific event into an eternal context. Myths are told to express realities beyond mere historical accounts. Many people see the early parts of the Bible as myths in this way.

Name

In the Bible, a name is more than just a way to identify someone; it expresses the essential nature, the true character of the person who bears it. When you know someone's name (or God's names), you know who he really is. Significant changes in a person are often marked by changing his name.

Parable

An extended metaphor or simile, often a little story that powerfully makes its point, usually through an ending that contains surprise and the reversal of what is expected. Parables were used masterfully by Jesus.

Parousia

A Greek word meaning "presence, arrival, or coming" that in the New Testament refers to the coming of Christ at the end of time (second coming).

Passover

A major Jewish festival commemorating the Exodus event when the angel of God "passed over" the Hebrews' houses marked with the blood of the lamb, thereby not killing their eldest sons along with the sons of the Egyptians. (This was the "plague" that caused the Pharaoh to let them leave.) Passover is also known as the Feast of Unleavened Bread, referring to the bread made in haste before they left. In Christianity, Christ becomes the Passover Lamb whose sacrifice frees humanity from the bondage of sin and restores oneness with God and with one another.

Peace

In Hebrew Scripture *shalom* means "whole," "well-being," and "harmony," expressing the ideal state of life in Israel. In Christian Scripture it is the coming of the reign of God through Christ with harmony, wholeness, and a new relationship with God.

Pentateuch

The first five and most important books of the Hebrew Bible; also known as the Five Books of Moses. These books contain the essential teachings of Judaism (the Law, Torah), the defining event (the Exodus), and the story of the formation of the Jewish people.

Pentecost

In Hebrew Scripture this term refers to the feast also known as Weeks that marked the end of the wheat harvest; later it was fifty days from the Sabbath following Passover (hence Pentecost). In Christian Scripture it is the day of the outpouring of the Spirit and the start of the growth of the Church (Acts 2), sometimes called "the birth day" of the church.

Pharisees

See Sadducees.

Prayer

Conversation with God or worship offered to God by individuals or groups with or without human or divine mediators. The principal kinds of prayer are: adoration, praise, thanksgiving, penitence (forgiveness), oblation (offering), intercession (on behalf of others), and petition (requests). The Lord's Prayer was given by Jesus to his disciples as a model for how to pray (the two versions are found in Matthew 6:9–13 and Luke 11:2–4).

Prophet, prophecy

In Hebrew Scripture the prophets analyzed events and people's behaviors, compared them to what was required by the Torah, and described the consequences (good if you followed the Law; bad if you did not). In Christian Scripture many of the prophecies of promise and hope in the Hebrew Bible were seen as pointing to Jesus as the Messiah. Like their Jewish predecessors, Christian prophets in the New Testament announced God's word as it was revealed to them in their particular situations (Acts 19:6; 21:9; 1 Corinthians 14:3ff.).

Reconciliation, reconcile

Coming to agreement or restoring a relationship after a disagreement or estrangement. In the Hebrew Bible we are estranged from God by breaking the Law and restored through the sacrificial system. In the New Testament reconciliation describes the changed relationship between God and us as a result of the life, death, and resurrection of Jesus Christ. God chooses to be reconciled to us—to bring us into relationship with God through Christ—out of love for us. We can choose to be reconciled or reject God's offer of reconciliation. Christians are called to be ministers of reconciliation, working to restore unity between God and others.

Redeem, redemption

In the Hebrew language it means buying back something that formerly belongs to the buyer. Or it may mean paying the price required to secure a benefit (as in buying a slave's freedom). Israel was redeemed by God, who delivered them from slavery. In Christian Scripture it refers to Jesus giving his life as a ransom for us, thus securing our salvation.

Repent

To change one's mind, to return and reorient one's whole life and personality. This includes leaving old behaviors, attitudes, and values and adopting a new way of being. The story of the prodigal son in Luke 15 portrays repentance. The word is also associated with feelings of regret and remorse.

Resurrection

In Christianity it refers to the event of Jesus Christ rising from the dead. Christian Scripture proclaims this and does not explain it, assuming it is a reality and mystery beyond human understanding. In biblical times the apostles were those who had seen it and could tell about it. Christians accept their witness as true.

Reveal, revelation

To unveil, uncover something. In the Bible, God chooses to reveal, to show God's self; this is the only way we know about God. God is revealed in God's acts in history, in the witness of the prophets, and for Christians, especially in Jesus Christ. Christians believe that God in Christ continues to be revealed to people through the Holy Spirit. The Book of Revelation tells about Christ's return.

Righteous, righteousness

Occasionally translated "justice," righteousness means right action and fair dealings. It involves the establishment of equal rights for all and suggests generosity and benevolence to the poor and helpless. In Christian Scripture, Paul uses it to mean the salvation that God accomplishes through Christ (Romans 3:21).

Sabbath

Based on a Hebrew verb that means "to cease," "to abstain," or "to be at an end," Sabbath refers to a cessation of work. It is the closing day of a seven-day week. For Jews the Sabbath begins at sunset on Friday and concludes on Saturday; it is a holy day when all physical labor is to cease and Jews gather in synagogues for worship and study. Most Christians worship on Sunday, celebrating Christ's resurrection from the dead which occurred on that day. At first Christians observed both the Jewish Sabbath and the Christian celebration. After 70 CE Jews and Christians separated and increasingly Christians observed Sunday as Resurrection Day *and* a sabbath.

Sacrifice

Literally, "to slaughter." In the Hebrew Bible the word often refers to animals that were killed and offered to God. These offerings were a way to enter into a relationship with God or to restore the relationship after wrongdoing. The sacrifices offered in the temple were accepted by God as payment for sins, as thank offerings, or as a way to commune with God. In the Christian Testament the word usually refers to Christ's sacrifice which is "once and for all" (see the Letter to the Hebrews) thus ending the need to repeat the temple sacrifices.

Sadducees and Pharisees

Sadducees were the priestly party in Judaism whose views and practices diverged sharply from those of the Pharisees, who were known for their devout faith and legalism. Pharisees believed that history was controlled by God, and believed in angels, resurrection, and an end time, when the Messiah would overthrow the Gentiles. Sadducees believed individuals had freedom to shape their own history, did not believe in angels, spirits, or the resurrection of the body. They believed that the soul died with the body.

Saint

The term refers to someone who is "holy" or "set apart" for God's use. In Hebrew Scripture it refers to the Hebrew people ("You are a people holy to the Lord your God . . ." [Deuteronomy 7:6]). In the New Testament it refers to Christian believers, who are "holy" by being "in Christ" (Philemon 1:1).

Sanctify, sanctification

The process of becoming or being made holy. In Hebrew Scripture holiness belongs to God, who can give it to people and things. According to Christian Scripture, Christians are holy by being "in Christ" and, at the same time, are constantly being made holy (being sanctified) by God in Christ.

Sanhedrin

The supreme Jewish council during postexilic times that had, at various times, legislative, executive, and judicatory functions. The high priest acted as president. It was this group that summoned Jesus to account for his actions and ultimately brought him to the Roman authorities for trial.

Save, salvation

"To save" meant to have the strength and ability to deliver someone (or oneself) from danger, evil, oppression, destruction, or brokenness. Salvation in the Bible was marked by victory, freedom, or wholeness. We look to God to save us, to free us from that which threatens to destroy us, and make us whole.

Savior

The one who saves. In the Hebrew Scriptures it often refers to kings or military leaders who rescue their people, usually on behalf of God, who was thought of as the Savior. In the New Testament it generally refers to Christ, the Savior of the world.

Scribes

A professional class of teachers of the Law in postexilic Judaism.

Scriptures

Holy writings or sacred texts accepted by a faith group as authoritative (having divine authority) because they are seen as inspired by God (even if written by humans, see 2 Timothy 3:16). Most religious groups have writings they accept as Scripture. Jews and Christians call their scriptures "the Bible" (meaning "the books").

Servant

One who serves; used to mean workers or slaves (who were the property of their masters). The subjects of a king or of state officials are "servants" as are those who worship a god (servants of Baal). Christ chose to take on the form of a "servant" (Philemon 2:7) in order to serve us. Christians "belong" to Christ and are called to serve Christ and one another.

Shema

The first words of Deuteronomy 6:4 ("Hear, O Israel, the Lord is our God . . . you must love the Lord your God with all your heart and with all your soul and with all your strength"). This is Judaism's primary confession of faith.

Sin

In the Hebrew Bible sin is primarily seen as breaking the covenant relationship between God and people. It is partly failing to miss a goal, partly going off from what is right (intentionally or unintentionally), and partly rebelling against a superior. Sin is also an attitude that leads to breaking or being unfaithful to God's covenant. Jesus emphasized the internal dynamics of sin and our relationship to God over the external "rules" of the religious leaders. Paul saw everyone as "missing the mark" in that we chronically fail to be who God created us to be, whether or not we know it. We can choose to break the relationship between God and us, between us and others. Or we can choose to be in relationship with God through Christ.

Spirit, Holy.

See Holy Spirit.

Spiritual gifts

Terms used in the New Testament for the special way in which God acts through a baptized Christian. Spiritual gifts include the gifts of wisdom, knowledge, faith, teaching, administration, healing, service, evangelism, miracles, tongues, and discernment. See 1 Corinthians 12:8–10, 28–30; Romans 12:6–8; Ephesians 4:11.

Suffer, suffering

To experience personal or corporate pain such as sickness, poverty, or oppression. In the Hebrew Scriptures suffering is largely seen as punishment for sin; this is challenged in Job. It is also seen as discipline that strengthens (Zechariah 13:9; Malachi 3:2ff.) or an offering of self that benefits someone else (Isaiah 52:12–53:12). The Christian Scriptures emphasize Jesus' suffering for us so we do not suffer the consequence of our sin and brokenness. Jesus did not see suffering as punishment (Matthew 5:45); Paul saw it as an opportunity for profound personal and spiritual growth (Romans 5:3).

Tabernacle

A portable sanctuary or holy place sometimes called the Tent of Meeting. Exodus 25–31 records God's instructions to Moses on building the tabernacle, which was to be God's dwelling place. It held the Ark of the Covenant and traveled with the Israelites through the wilderness period. It was stationed in several places in Canaan before being replaced by Solomon's temple.

Temple of Jerusalem

Solomon, Zerubbabel, and Herod built three temples on the same site in Jerusalem; this site is now occupied by the Muslim shrine, the Dome of the Rock (Qubbet es-Sakhra). The temple in the Hebrew Bible is the place where God is present to the people who come to worship and where sacrifices and prayers can restore the people to relationship with God. The last temple in Jerusalem was destroyed as a consequence of a revolt against Rome in 70 CE. Jews still visit the remains of the temple's western wall as a most holy site. Jesus worshipped at the temple, predicted its destruction, and condemned those who used it for commerce. At his trial one of the charges against him was that he claimed he could pull down the temple and rebuild it in three days (Matthew 26:61).

Tempt, temptation

In modern English the verb largely means "to entice." In the Bible it means "to prove or to test" as in Satan testing Jesus in the wilderness (Matthew 4:1–11; Luke 4:1–13). Paul wrote the church at Corinth that "God will not let you be tested [tempted] beyond your strength" (1 Corinthians 10:13b).

Thanksgiving

In the Hebrew Scriptures thanksgiving includes praising, blessing, or acknowledging one's indebtedness to God. In Christian

Scripture and in the church today the great act of thanksgiving centers around the Eucharist (a Greek word which means "thanksgiving" and which refers to Christian celebration of Christ's life, death, and resurrection). At the Passover meal with his disciples, Jesus, following the usual Jewish customs, "blessed" the bread and wine by giving thanks. See also Bless.

Torah

The Hebrew word *torah* means "instruction," which includes teaching through specific commandments and telling stories. In Judaism it refers to the first five books of the Bible—Genesis, Exodus, Leviticus, Numbers, and Deuteronomy; these books are also called the Pentateuch or the Five Books of Moses. The Torah tells the story of the relationship between God and humanity which is expressed in and defined by the covenants between God and human beings. The three primary covenants in the Torah are the Noahaic covenant (Genesis 9), the Abrahamic covenant (Genesis 15 and 17), and the Mosaic covenant, sometimes called the Israelite covenant or the covenant of Sinai (Exodus 19–20). The Torah is the core of the Hebrew Bible—everything else is built around it and the covenants in it.

Truth

Truth is a quality of God; it means reliability, dependableness, and ability to perform what is required. For the Hebrews, when God required "truth" from people it meant that they were to do God's will as revealed in the Law. In the Christian Scriptures the Greek concept of "the actual state of affairs rather than a lie or a rumor" is combined with the broader Hebrew concept (see Romans 3:3–7). Sometimes truth meant reality as revealed by Christ (unlike that presented by others). In John's Gospel, truth is what has been made known of God's being in and through Jesus.

Word

In Hebrew, *word* means any spoken speech; it was understood in biblical times that words had a power of their own to cause action. So, for example, God's Word accomplished what it declared (Isaiah 55:11). In the New Testament God's Word becomes Jesus (the Word became "flesh," John 1:1–14). Christians also refer to the Bible or passages in it as "God's Word."

Worship, liturgy

Taken from the Hebrew word which means "to labor" or "to serve," these related words refer to "serving God" in rituals (specific prayers, songs, and actions). In the Christian Scriptures there is an emphasis on worship as adoring and loving God (shown by devotion to God and by serving one's neighbor). The rituals are to help us do that, but any act of love done as a service to God can be an act of worship.

Yahweh

The accepted pronunciation of the four consonants of the Israelite name for God (YHWH) which was originally written without vowels. After the exile (538 BCE) YHWH was not used lest the sacred name be profaned; words such as *Adonai* ("Lord") were substituted. Jehovah is an artificial name that arose out of the tradition of putting the vowels for *Adonai* into the name YHWH to indicate that it was to be verbalized as Adonai.

Zion

A term first applied to the hill now occupied by Jerusalem, then to Jerusalem itself or to the temple there.

TOOLS FOR FURTHER STUDY

Bible Translations and Paraphrases

Many people automatically think of the King James Version (KJV) when they think of the Bible. Until recent years it was the most common English translation and it is still preferred by many, especially for reading aloud (it uses beautiful poetic language). However, its use of Elizabethan English makes understanding some portions difficult. In recent years new translations of the Bible have appeared that are much more readable than the KJV. They also incorporate new scholarship not available to translators in 1611.

Today the New Revised Standard Version (NRSV) is very popular. It is often acknowledged as the most accurate, readable, and authoritative translation. It incorporates the most recent research and is rapidly replacing its predecessor, the Revised Standard Version (RSV). The New Jerusalem Bible (NJB) and the New English Version (NEV) are also popular current translations. The New International Version (NIV) represents more conservative scholarship, while the New American Bible is the American Roman Catholic version of the Bible. The Complete Parallel Bible (Oxford) offers these four translations side by side. The Tanakh, or the Holy Scripture, is a 1988 combination of the prior translations of the three sections of the Hebrew

Bible (Torah [Law], Nebi'im [Prophets], and Ketubim [Writings]), thus TNK. This English translation was done under the auspices of the Jewish Publication Society.

The repetition of the words "new" and "revised" gives you a clue that each of these translations has been updated in recent years. One of the reasons for this is the discovery of the Dead Sea Scrolls in 1947, which gave us some of the oldest copies of the biblical texts. As these scrolls are translated, they give us new information about the original texts.

There is nothing that makes one translation more "holy" than another. Each has been translated from Hebrew or Greek into modern languages as they were spoken a couple of hundred years ago (KJV) or the language we use today (NRSV). Each group of translators has respectfully translated the texts, using the current knowledge and its best efforts at being accurate. The problem is that this is a difficult task and there is no perfect way to do it. Scholars have different opinions about what a word means. Our knowledge about what a word means changes as we discover more about the original language and texts. And our language—the way we say things—changes as well. So different versions say the same thing different ways.

It is good to use more than one version if you are going to study the Bible so you can see what the different scholars have done. Remember also these distinctions: Translations try to translate faithfully the words of the ancient texts; paraphrases reword the Bible to make it more understandable. Paraphrases convey the theological orientation of the writer (liberal, conservative, etc.). This often distorts the original texts by adding interpretation and varied meanings. Most paraphrases are therefore not especially useful for study purposes.

Study Bibles

The HarperCollins Study Bible
New Revised Standard Version with the Apocryphal/Deuterocanonical Books (HarperCollins Publishers, 1993)

Make sure you get the HarperCollins study version (there
    is a Harper version and a nonstudy version); the other
    versions do not have introductions to the books or the
    extensive footnotes. The study version has some excel-
    lent maps and charts scattered throughout and at the
    end. One chart gives the parallel passages in the four
    Gospels, eliminating the need to buy a separate book
    (see Gospel parallels below).

The Oxford Study Bible
The Revised English Bible with Apocrypha (Oxford
    University Press, 1992)
This study Bible includes maps, footnotes, a twenty-two-
    page guide to the biblical world, introductions to the
    books, and articles that highlight particular sections.
    Again, make sure to get the study version. The Oxford
    annotated is available on CD-ROM.

The New Student Bible
New International Version or New Revised
    Standard Version (Zondervan Bible Publishers, 1994)
This study Bible, appropriate for teens and young adults,
    features a student-oriented subject guide, book intro-
    ductions, "Highlight" and "Insight" sections for back-
    ground and a Bible story directory.

The NIV Study Bible
New International Version (Zondervan Bible Publishers,
    1985)
This Bible contains nearly twenty thousand study notes
    located on the same pages as the verse they explain.
    Also included: cross-reference system with 100,000 en-
    tries, a concordance of 35,000 entries, charts, maps,
    essays, and comprehensive indexes. The notes take a
    more theologically conservative stance than many
    other study Bibles.

Collections of Texts

Gospel Parallels (Thomas Nelson Publishers, 1962)
Burton H. Throckmorton, Jr.
Gospel parallels show the four Gospels on one page so
   you can see the similarities and differences.

The Other Bible (Harper & Row, 1984)
Willis Barnstone, editor
Collection of ancient Jewish and Christian texts excluded
   from the official canon.

Commentaries

Commentaries are books that "comment on" a Scripture
passage. You can get commentaries on each book in the
Bible, which is most helpful if you are doing in-depth
study of a particular book. Those written specifically for
preachers often make contemporary connections and are
useful to nonpreachers as well. If you're just starting to
explore the Bible, you might begin with a general commentary such as *The Interpreter's One-Volume Commentary
on the Bible.*

The Interpreter's One-Volume Commentary on the Bible
   (Abingdon Press, 1971)
Written by many of the best biblical scholars, this handy
   commentary gives information about every passage in
   the Bible in one concise book. Readable and easy to
   use.

Harper's Bible Commentary (Harper San Francisco, 1988)
James L. Mays, editor
Easy to use introduction to the Bible. Good for beginners.

Eerdmans' Handbook to the Bible (Eerdmans, 1983)
Classic commentary on the Bible for the common reader.
   A bit dated.

Preaching the Revised Common Lectionary (Abingdon
Press, 1992)

Marion Soards et al., editors

A twelve-volume set of commentaries (expensive) with
about ten pages on each set of weekly lessons in the
Revised Common Lectionary (RCL). Designed for
preachers but a good resource for individuals or groups
using the RCL (see pages 193–245).

Texts for Preaching: A Lectionary Commentary Based on
the NRSV (Westminster/John Knox Press, 1994)

Charles B. Courar et al., editors

This commentary comes in three volumes (one for each
year of the lectionary) and is designed to help preachers with the lectionary texts assigned for each week. It
would be most useful to those studying scripture texts
using the lectionary cycle.

The New Jerome Biblical Commentary (Prentice-Hall,
1990)

Raymond E. Brown, Joseph A. Fitzmeyer, and Roland E.
Murphy, editors

Two volumes in one. Well-respected commentary with official Roman Catholic *Imprimatur* (approval); written
by some of the best Roman Catholic biblical scholars.

Interpretation (Westminster/John Knox Press, 1984–   )

A multi-volume commentary by renowned biblical scholars on the books of the Bible.

Westminster Guide to the Bible (Westminster/John Knox
Press, 1984–   )

Commentary by groups of books: Pentateuch, Prophets,
etc.

The Women's Bible Commentary (Westminster/John
Knox Press, 1992)

Carol A. Newsom and Sharon H. Ringe, editors

Includes a series of articles on various books of the Bible from the perspective of women scholars.

Searching the Scriptures (Crossroad, 1994)
Elisabeth Schussler Fiorenza with Shelly Matthews
A feminist commentary that includes extensive bibliographical references.

The Illustrated Guide to the Bible (Oxford University Press, 1995)
J. R. Porter
Looks at the narratives in the Bible from historical, social, archaeological, and mythological perspectives. Summarizes each book of the Bible.

Bible Dictionaries

Bible dictionaries are just what you'd imagine from the name—books that define words in the Bible. But they usually contain more than simple definitions; they include articles about concepts and have lots of other useful material.

The Interpreter's Dictionary of the Bible: Volumes 1–4 (Abingdon Press, 1962)
Supplementary Volume (Abingdon Press, 1976)
More than eight thousand key concepts in the Bible discussed in detail; includes pronunciation guide, cross references, and major articles. Maps, photos, and full-length articles on each book of the Bible also included. Five hefty but valuable books. A bit dated; watch for an updated version.

The Oxford Companion to the Bible (Oxford University Press, 1993)
Edited by Bruce M. Metzger and Michael D. Coogan
A comprehensive one-volume guide to people, places, and events in the Bible which includes a broad range of arti-

cles and twenty-eight pages of maps. Includes all of the books considered canonical by any religious community. Addresses modern issues such as ecology, human sexuality, and the role of women.

HarperCollins Bible Dictionary (Harper San Francisco, 1996)
Paul J. Achtemeier, editor
One-volume, easy-to-use dictionary, completely revised form of the 1985 *Harper's Bible Dictionary.*

The Anchor Bible Dictionary (Doubleday, 1992)
David Noel Freedman, Editor
An up-to-date six-volume dictionary covering almost every conceivable biblical subject, with maps, illustrations, and bibliography. This is the most current and comprehensive Bible dictionary available (hardcover and CD-ROM).

NIV Compact Dictionary of the Bible (Zondervan Publishing House, 1989)
An accessible, readable guide to many biblical words and concepts. Based on terms used in the New International Version (NIV) of the Bible.

Concordances

Concordances are books that help you find a passage when you can remember only a couple of words. They list passages by key words, enabling you to see all the passages that use a word you might want to focus on in a study session. These are big books with tiny print and a high price tag. Look for one in a library or at a church or synagogue. Also, many of the current electronic Bibles allow you to do word searches, essentially eliminating the need for these books.

The Concise Concordance to the New Revised Standard Version (Oxford University Press, 1993)

NIV Complete Concordance (Zondervan Publishing, 1981)

NRSV Exhaustive Concordance (Thomas Nelson Publishers, 1991)

Strong's Concordance to the Bible (Abingdon Press, 1970)

Young's Analytical Concordance to the Bible (KJV) (Wm. B. Eerdmans Publishing Company, 1972)

Atlases

These books provide multiple, detailed maps that help you find your way around the biblical landscape.

Oxford Bible Atlas (Oxford University Press, 1962)
Herbert G. May, editor
Full-color maps of biblical lands with many helpful illustrations.

The Harper Atlas of the Bible (Harper & Row, 1987)
James B. Pritchard, editor
Helpful atlas with ample illustrations and maps.

Computer Resources

There are countless computer resources, including all versions of the Bible, concordances, dictionaries, Bible study programs, maps, and games. The following items represent only a very small selection. For reviews of existing programs and information about new programs, consult one of the magazines or books that review computer resources.

WORDsearch (NavPress)
Comes with your choice of translations of the Bible and

allows you to search for keywords, wild cards, and topics and to transfer texts into your word processor. Add-ons include a Bible study lesson maker, maps, Scofield Outlines, Strong's Ties to the Greek and Hebrew, a Bible dictionary, cross references, Matthew Henry's Six Volume Commentary on the Whole Bible, Teacher's Commentary, A. T. Robertson's Word Pictures in the New Testament, Life Application Notes, parallel passages, and Hannah's Outlines of every book, chapter, and cluster of verses.

QuickVerse (Parsons Technology)

Allows you to search for words or phrases, cut and paste into your word processor; your choice of translations. Add-ons include Strong's Concordance with Hebrew and Greek Dictionaries, New Scofield Study Bible, Holman Bible Dictionary, Matthew Henry's Concise Six Volume Commentary on the Whole Bible, Believer's or Ryrie Study Bible, and interactive maps with database of every place named in the Bible.

Logos Bible Software (Logos Research Systems)

Four CDs with different software combinations, including various translations, original-language texts and tools; Harper's and New Bible Dictionaries; Bible Knowledge Commentary, Harper's, Jerome's, or Matthew Henry's Six Volume Commentary on the Whole Bible; topical Bible; maps; devotional texts; MIDI hymns; original language texts and tools. A basic package is available with add-ons as desired. Also available in Chinese, Japanese, and Korean, with other languages in the works.

Bible Explorer for Windows (Epiphany Software)

A CD-ROM program with translations, commentaries, devotional and other Christian literature, dictionaries, maps, atlases, photographs, art, topic and word studies. Other add-ons in future releases. Lower cost than most.

TIME
LINE

BIBLICAL EVENTS	EVENTS IN THE ANCIENT WORLD	HISTORIC PERIODS	
CREATION ACCOUNTS		Paleolithic Period	before 14,000 BCE
		Mesolithic Period	14,000 to 8,500 BCE
	◆ Beginning of civilization *First agricultural communities, appearance of pottery*	Neolithic Period	8,500 to 4,300 BCE
NOAH AND THE ARK	◆ Increased cultural contact *Communities innovate and advance*	Chalcolithic Period	4,300 to 3,300 BCE
	◆ Emergence of cities and political dynasties *Mesopotamia—Ur, Sumerians, Akkadians Anatolia—Early Hittite Kingdom Egypt—Early Kingdom*	Early Bronze Age (Widespread use of bronze)	3,300 to 2,300 BCE
		Transition Period (EB/MB)	2,300 to 2,000 BCE
PATRIARCHAL AGE **ABRAHAM, ISAAC,** **JACOB, JOSEPH**	◆ International relations between large city-states (trade, commerce, war) *Mesopotamia—Hammurabi, Mari, Babylon Anatolia—Early Hittite Kingdom, Mitanni Palestine—Amorites and Sea People settle here Egypt—Middle Kingdom*	Middle Bronze Age	2,000 to 1,550 BCE

Date	Event	Description	Age	Period
	HEBREWS IN EGYPT	◆ Established powers vie for regional control *Mesopotamia—Cassite dynasty and period of decline* *Anatolia—Mitanni, Arameans, New Hittite Kingdom*	Late Bronze Age	1,550 to 1,200 BCE
		Palestine—Local city-states and nomads in conflict, under Egyptian control		
	MOSES, AARON			
	THE EXODUS (1250?)	*Egypt—Hyksos* *West Mediterranean coast—fall of Crete, Mycenean culture*		
1200	WILDERNESS WANDERINGS	◆ Rise and fall of international empires	Iron Age	1,200 to 332 BCE
1150	ISRAELITE CONQUEST AND SETTLEMENT (JOSHUA)			
1100	PERIOD OF THE JUDGES (GIDEON, SAMSON)	*Western Mediterranean coast—Trojan War (?)*		
1050	SAUL (c. 1025–1005) SAMUEL	*Beginning of united monarchy in Israel*		

	BIBLICAL EVENTS	EVENTS IN THE ANCIENT WORLD	HISTORIC PERIODS
			1200 to 332 BCE
1000	DAVID (c. 1005–965)		Iron Age
950	SOLOMON (c. 965–925)	End of united monarchy, north (Israel) and south (Judah) split	
	REHOBOAM I (924–907) King of Judah	Egypt—Shishak of Egypt leads military expedition into Palestine (919)	
	JEROBOAM I (924–903) King of Israel		
900	ERA OF KINGS	Mesopotamia—Neo-Assyrian Empire (c. 900–609)	
850	PROPHETS ACTIVE (ELIJAH, ELISHA, ISAIAH, JEREMIAH, EZEKIEL, etc.)		
800		Western Mediterranean coast—Homer, first Olympic Games	
750	END OF NORTHERN KINGDOM (722)	Samaria, capital of Israel, falls to Assyrian king Sargon II (722)	
700			

650	*Mesopotamia—Babylonian Empire* (c. 626–539)
600	**JEHOIACHIN SURRENDERS JERUSALEM TO THE BABYLONIANS AND IS TAKEN INTO EXILE (597)**
	END OF SOUTHERN KINGDOM (586) — *Nebuchadnezzar captures and destroys Jerusalem (586)* Many of Judah's Inhabitants Exiled to Babylon
550	**UNDER CYRUS, JERUSALEM TEMPLE REBUILT** — *Mesopotamia—Persian Empire (c. 538–330) ruled by Cyrus II*
500	**EZRA RETURNS TO JERUSALEM (458?)** — *Greece—Herodotus*
450	**NEHEMIAH SENT TO OVERSEE JERUSALEM (445)**

	BIBLICAL EVENTS	EVENTS IN THE ANCIENT WORLD	HISTORIC PERIODS	
400		*Decline of Athens*		
350		◆ Alexander the Great conquers the east	Hellenistic Period	332 to 63 BCE
300				
250		*Ptolemaic rule in Palestine*	Carthaginian Wars (264–201)	
200	**MACCABEAN REVOLT** (168–164)	*Seleucid rule in Palestine*	Macedonian Wars (215–168)	
150				
100		◆ Pompey conquers the East	Roman period	63 BCE to 324 CE
50		Caesar Roman emperor *Cleopatra, Marc Antony in Egypt* *Octavian becomes "Augustus"*		
1 BCE	**JESUS BORN 4 BCE**	*Herod the Great king of Palestine (38–4 BCE)*		

1 CE	JESUS CRUCIFIED 30 CE Birth of the Church
50	PAUL WRITES TO THE EARLY CHURCH
	Destruction of Jerusalem by Romans (70)
100	NEW TESTAMENT WRITINGS COMPLETE
	Bar Kokhba Revolt (132–35)

MAPS

THE GEOGRAPHY OF THE ANCIENT NEAR EAST

ARAL SEA

CASPIAN

SEA

CAUCASUS MTS.

URARTU
(ARMENIA)

ALBORZ MTS.
(ELBURZ MTS.)

Nineveh

MESOPOTAMIA
(IRAQ)

Ecbatana

ZAGROS MTS.

PERSIA
(IRAN)

FERTILE

CRESCENT

R. Euphrates

R. Tigris

Babylon

Ur

Persepolis

ARABIAN

DESERT

PERSIAN

GULF

GULF
OF
OMAN

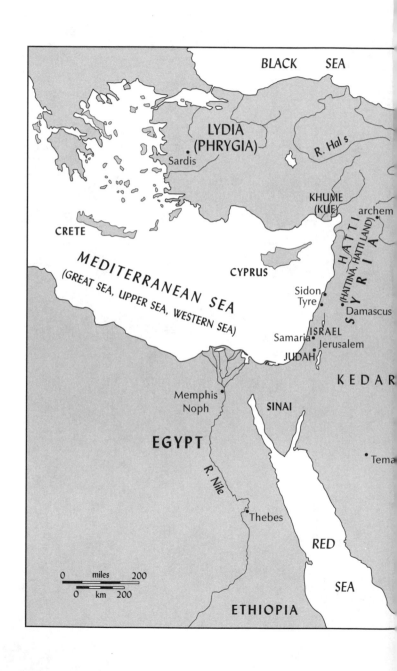

ASSYRIAN (900–609 BCE) AND BABYLONIAN (626–539 BCE) EMPIRES

URARTU
(ARARAT)

CASPIAN

SEA

MANNAI
(MINNI)

ASSYRIA

aran

Nineveh

MEDIA

Asshur

R. Tigris

Ecbatana

R. Euphrates

Babylon

BABYLONIA
(CHALDEA)

Susa

ELAM

Erech (Uruk)

Ur

PERSIA

PERSIAN GULF
(LOWER SEA, EASTERN SEA)

ARABIA

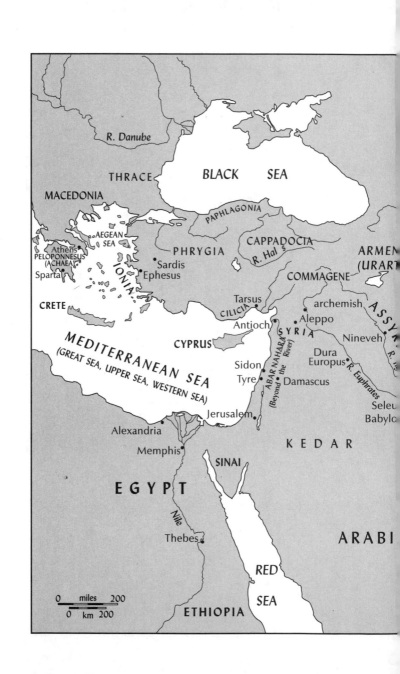

R. Danube

THRACE

MACEDONIA

BLACK   SEA

PAPHLAGONIA

AEGEAN
SEA

Athens
PELOPONNESUS
(ACHAEA)

Sparta

IONIA

PHRYGIA

Sardis
Ephesus

R. Halys

CAPPADOCIA

ARMEN
(URART

COMMAGENE

CRETE

CYPRUS

Tarsus

CILICIA

archemish

ASSYR

Antioch

SYRIA

Aleppo

Nineveh

R.

MEDITERRANEAN SEA
(GREAT SEA, UPPER SEA, WESTERN SEA)

Sidon
Tyre

ABAR NAHARA
(Beyond the River)

Dura
Europus

R. Euphrates

Damascus

Seleu
Babylo

Jerusalem

Alexandria

KEDAR

Memphis

SINAI

EGYPT

Nile

Thebes

ARABI

RED

SEA

0   miles   200
0   km   200

ETHIOPIA

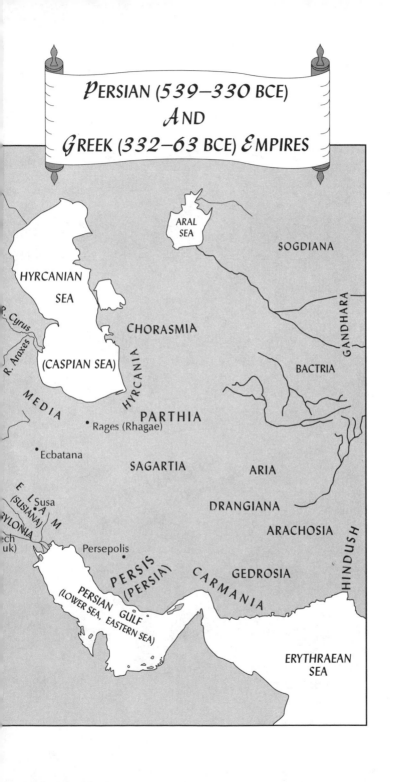

PERSIAN (539–330 BCE) AND GREEK (332–63 BCE) EMPIRES

ARAL SEA

SOGDIANA

HYRCANIAN SEA

R. Cyrus

R. Araxes

CHORASMIA

(CASPIAN SEA)

GANDHARA

BACTRIA

MEDIA

HYRCANIA

PARTHIA

• Rages (Rhagae)

• Ecbatana

SAGARTIA

ARIA

E L Susa
A (SUSIANA)
BYLONIA M
ch
uk)

DRANGIANA

ARACHOSIA

• Persepolis

PERSIS (PERSIA)

CARMANIA

GEDROSIA

HINDUSH

PERSIAN GULF
(LOWER SEA, EASTERN SEA)

ERYTHRAEAN SEA

ROMAN EMPIRE
(63 BCE– 324 CE)

SCYTHIANS

BOSPORAN
KINGDOM

CASPIAN
SEA

BLACK   SEA
(Pontus Euxinus)

COLCHIS

eraclea

BITHYNIA and PONTUS

Ancyra

KINGDOM
OF
ARMENIA

R. Araxes

LESSER
ARMENIA

S
Y
R
I
A

GALATIA

R. Halys

CAPPADOCIA

PISIDIA

PAMPHYLIA

Tarsus

CILICIA

COMMAGENE

Edessa

PARTHIAN

EMPIRE

CYPRUS

Antioch

R. Orontes

SYRIA

Dura-Europus

Sidon
Tyre

R. Jordan

Damascus

PALESTINE

R. Euphrates

Seleucia

Jerusalem
JUDEA

NABATAEAN KINGDOM

Babylon

R. Tigris

Memphis

Nile

Petra

ARABIAN

DESERT

RED SEA

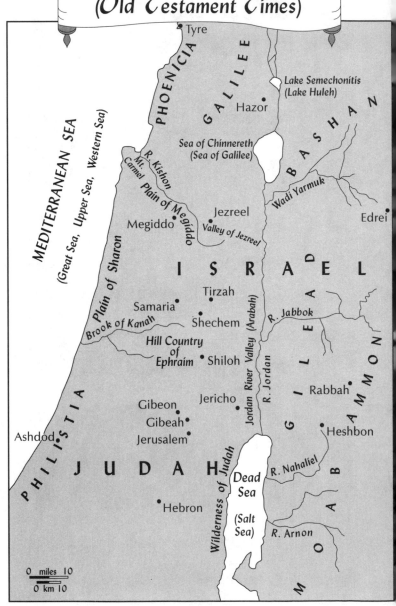

PALESTINE
FROM 1200–100 BCE
(Old Testament Times)

Tyre

PHOENICIA

GALILEE

Lake Semechonitis
(Lake Huleh)

Hazor

BASHAN

Sea of Chinnereth
(Sea of Galilee)

MEDITERRANEAN SEA
(Great Sea, Upper Sea, Western Sea)

R. Kishon

Mt. Carmel

Plain of Megiddo

Wadi Yarmuk

Jezreel

Megiddo

Valley of Jezreel

Edrei

Plain of Sharon

I S R A E L

G I L E A D

Tirzah

Samaria

Brook of Kanah

Shechem

R. Jabbok

Hill Country
of Ephraim

Shiloh

AMMON

PHILISTIA

Gibeon

Jericho

Rabbah

Gibeah

Jerusalem

Jordan River Valley (Arabah)

R. Jordan

Heshbon

Ashdod

J U D A H

Wilderness of Judah

R. Nahaliel

M O A B

Dead
Sea
(Salt
Sea)

Hebron

R. Arnon

0   miles   10

0   km   10

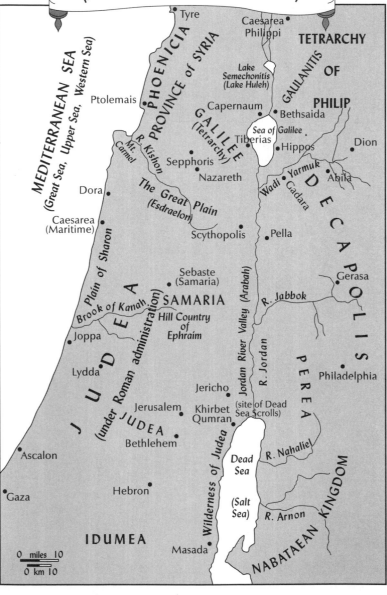

PALESTINE
FROM 4 BCE–100 CE
(New Testament Times)

Tyre

Caesarea
Philippi

TETRARCHY

Lake
Semechonitis
(Lake Huleh)

OF

PHOENICIA

PROVINCE of SYRIA

GALILEE
(Tetrarchy)

GAULANITIS

PHILIP

Capernaum

Bethsaida

Sea of Galilee

MEDITERRANEAN SEA
(Great Sea, Upper Sea, Western Sea)

Ptolemais

Tiberias

Hippos

Dion

Mt. Carmel

R. Kishon

Sepphoris

Nazareth

Wadi   Yarmuk

Abila

D E C A P O L I S

Dora

The Great Plain
(Esdraelon)

Gadara

Caesarea
(Maritime)

Scythopolis

Pella

Plain of Sharon

Sebaste
(Samaria)

Gerasa

Brook of Kanah

SAMARIA

(under Roman administration)

Hill Country
of
Ephraim

R. Jabbok

Joppa

P E R E A

Lydda

Jericho

Jordan River Valley (Arabah)

Philadelphia

J U D E A

Jerusalem

Khirbet
Qumran

(site of Dead
Sea Scrolls)

R. Jordan

JUDEA

Ascalon

Bethlehem

Dead
Sea

R. Nahaliel

Wilderness of Judea

Gaza

Hebron

(Salt
Sea)

NABATAEAN KINGDOM

R. Arnon

0 miles 10

IDUMEA

Masada

0 km 10